Anonymous

The book of the Gospels,

According to the use of the United Church of England and Ireland

throughout the year

Anonymous

The book of the Gospels,
According to the use of the United Church of England and Ireland throughout the year

ISBN/EAN: 9783337714666

Printed in Europe, USA, Canada, Australia, Japan

Cover: Foto ©ninafisch / pixelio.de

More available books at **www.hansebooks.com**

THE BOOK

OF

THE GOSPELS,

ACCORDING TO THE USE OF THE

UNITED CHURCH OF ENGLAND AND IRELAND

THROUGHOUT THE YEAR.

LONDON:

SOLD BY

THOMAS BOSWORTH, 215, REGENT STREET.

1867.

Introductory Note.

HEN *shall he* [the Priest-Celebrant or Minister] *read the Gospel, the People all standing up, saying,* "The Holy Gospel is written in the — Chapter of — beginning at the — verse." *Rubric in the Book of Common Prayer.*

Direction for Singing the Gospel.

The Gospel admits of an inflection from the dominant to the third below, *e. g.* Fa to Re, on the fourth* syllable from a period;† also before an interrogation, as in the Epistle; and one on the fifth syllable from the end,‡ as *e. g.* in the Gospel for Christmas-Day.

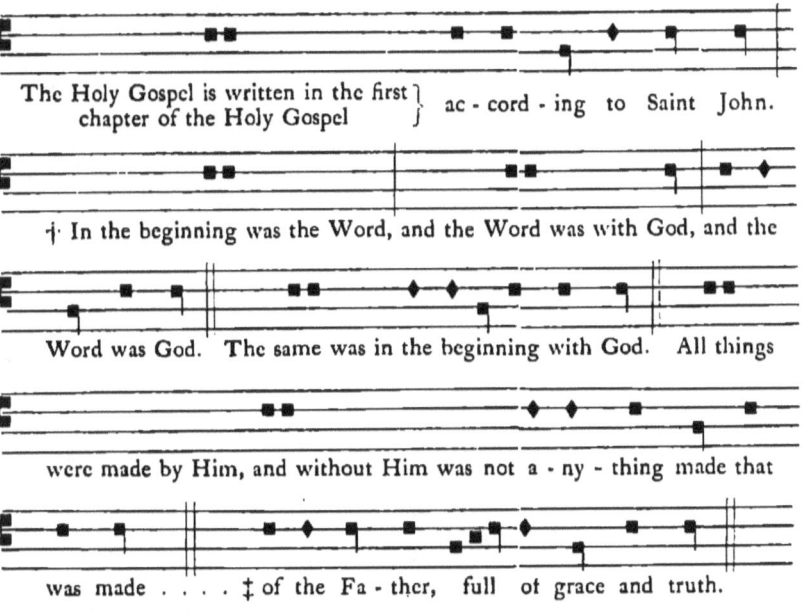

The Holy Gospel is written in the first chapter of the Holy Gospel ac-cord-ing to Saint John.

† In the beginning was the Word, and the Word was with God, and the Word was God. The same was in the beginning with God. All things were made by Him, and without Him was not a-ny-thing made that was made . . . . ‡ of the Fa-ther, full of grace and truth.

* This rule cannot always be rigidly kept; when not followed, the inflection should be made on the most important word or syllable of a word nearest the fourth.

Laus Tibi Christe.

Contents.

HE Sundays in Advent.
Christmas Day.
Saint Stephen's Day.
Saint John the Evangelist's Day.
The Innocents' Day.
The Sunday after Christmas Day.
The Circumcision of Christ.
The Epiphany.
The Sundays after the Epiphany.
The Sunday called Septuagesima.
The Sunday called Sexagesima.
The Sunday called Quinquagesima.
Ash Wednesday.
The Sundays in Lent.
The Sunday next before Easter.
The Monday before Easter.
The Tuesday before Easter.
The Wednesday before Easter.
The Thursday before Easter.
Good Friday.
Easter Even.
Easter Day.
The Monday in Easter Week.
The Tuesday in Easter Week.
The Sundays after Easter.
The Ascension-Day.
The Sunday after Ascension-Day.
Whitsun-Day.

The Monday in Whitsun-Week.
The Tuesday in Whitsun-Week.
Trinity Sunday.
The Sundays after Trinity.
Saint Andrew's Day.
Saint Thomas the Apostle.
The Conversion of Saint Paul.
The Purification of Saint Mary the Virgin.
Saint Matthias's Day.
The Annunciation of the Blessed Virgin Mary.
Saint Mark's Day.
Saint Philip and Saint James's Day.
Saint Barnabas the Apostle.
Saint John Baptist's Day.
Saint Peter's Day.
Saint James the Apostle.
Saint Bartholomew the Apostle.
Saint Matthew the Apostle.
Saint Michael and all Angels.
Saint Luke the Evangelist.
Saint Simon and Saint Jude, Apostles.
All Saints' Day.
At Funerals.
The Ordering of Deacons.
The Ordering of Priests.
The Consecration of Bishops.
The Queen's Accession.

The Book of the Gospels.

❧ The First Sunday in Advent.

St. Matth. xxi. 1.

HEN they drew nigh unto Jerusalem, and were come to Bethphage, unto the mount of Olives, then sent Jesus two disciples, saying unto them, Go into the village over against you, and straightway ye shall find an ass tied, and a colt with her: loose them, and bring them unto Me. And if any man say ought unto you, ye shall say, The Lord hath need of them; and straightway he will send them. All this was done, that it might be fulfilled which was spoken by the Prophet, saying, Tell ye the daughter of Sion, Behold, thy King cometh unto thee, meek, and sitting upon an ass, and a colt the foal of an ass. And the disciples went, and did as Jesus commanded them; and brought the ass, and the colt, and put on them their clothes, and they set Him thereon. And a very great multitude spread their garments in the way; others cut down branches from the trees, and strawed them in the way. And the multitudes that went before, and that followed, cried, saying, Hosanna to the Son of David; Blessed is He that cometh in the Name of the Lord; Hosanna in the highest. And when He was come into Jerusalem, all the city was moved, saying, Who is this? And the multitude said, This is

The Book of the Gospels.

Jesus the Prophet of Nazareth of Galilee. And Jesus went into the temple of God, and cast out all them that sold and bought in the temple; and overthrew the tables of the moneychangers, and the seats of them that sold doves; and said unto them, It is written, My house shall be called the house of prayer; but ye have made it a den of thieves.

¶ The Second Sunday in Advent.

St. Luke xxi. 25.

AND there shall be signs in the sun, and in the moon, and in the stars; and upon the earth distress of nations, with perplexity, the sea and the waves roaring; men's hearts failing them for fear, and for looking after those things which are coming on the earth: for the powers of heaven shall be shaken. And then shall they see the Son of Man coming in a cloud with power and great glory. And when these things begin to come to pass, then look up, and lift up your heads; for your redemption draweth nigh. And He spake to them a parable, Behold the fig-tree, and all the trees; when they now shoot forth, ye see and know of your own selves that summer is now nigh at hand. So likewise ye, when ye see these things come to pass, know ye that the Kingdom of God is nigh at hand. Verily I say unto you, This generation shall not pass away, till all be fulfilled: heaven and earth shall pass away; but My Words shall not pass away.

The Book of the Gospels.

¶ The Third Sunday in Advent.

St. Matth. xi. 2.

OW when John had heard in the prison the works of Christ, he sent two of his disciples, and said unto Him, Art Thou He that should come, or do we look for another? Jesus answered and said unto them, Go and shew John again those things which ye do hear and see: The blind receive their sight, and the lame walk, the lepers are cleansed, and the deaf hear, the dead are raised up, and the poor have the Gospel preached to them: And blessed is he whosoever shall not be offended in Me. And as they departed, Jesus began to say unto the multitudes concerning John, What went ye out into the wilderness to see? a reed shaken with the wind? But what went ye out for to see? a man clothed in soft raiment? behold, they that wear soft clothing are in kings' houses. But what went ye out for to see? a prophet? yea, I say unto you, and more than a prophet. For this is he of whom it is written, Behold, I send My messenger before Thy Face, which shall prepare Thy Way before Thee.

¶ The Fourth Sunday in Advent.

St. John i. 19.

HIS is the record of John, when the Jews sent Priests and Levites from Jerusalem to ask him, Who art thou? And he confessed, and denied not; but confessed, I am not the Christ. And they asked him, What then? Art thou Elias? And he saith, I am not. Art thou that Prophet? And he answered, No. Then said they unto him, Who

The Book of the Gospels.

art thou? that we may give an answer to them that sent us. What sayest thou of thyself? He said, I am the voice of one crying in the wilderness, Make straight the Way of the Lord, as said the prophet Esaias. And they which were sent were of the Pharisees. And they asked him, and said unto him, Why baptizest thou then, if thou be not that Christ, nor Elias, neither that Prophet? John answered them, saying, I baptize with water: but there standeth One among you, Whom ye know not: He it is Who coming after me is preferred before me, Whose shoe's latchet I am not worthy to unloose. These things were done in Bethabara beyond Jordan, where John was baptizing.

THE NATIVITY OF OUR LORD,

OR THE BIRTH-DAY OF CHRIST, COMMONLY CALLED

Christmas-Day.

St. John i. 1.

IN the beginning was the Word, and the Word was with God, and the Word was God. The Same was in the beginning with God. All things were made by Him; and without Him was not anything made that was made. In Him was life, and the life was the Light of men. And the Light shineth in darkness, and the darkness comprehended it not. There was a man sent from God, whose name was John. The same came for a witness, to bear witness of the Light, that all men through him might believe. He was not that Light, but was sent to bear witness of that Light. That was the True Light, Which lighteth every man that cometh into the world. He was in the world, and the world was made by Him, and the world knew Him

The Book of the Gospels.

not. He came unto His own, and His own received Him not. But as many as received Him, to them gave He power to become the sons of God, even to them that believe on His Name: which were born, not of blood, nor of the will of the flesh, nor of the will of man, but of God. And The Word was made Flesh, and dwelt among us (and we beheld His glory, the glory as of the Only-Begotten of the Father) full of grace and truth.

¶ St. Stephen's Day.

St. Matth. xxiii. 34.

BEHOLD, I send unto you prophets, and wise men, and scribes; and some of them ye shall kill and crucify; and some of them shall ye scourge in your synagogues, and persecute them from city to city; that upon you may come all the righteous blood shed upon the earth, from the blood of righteous Abel unto the blood of Zacharias, son of Barachias, whom ye slew between the temple and the altar. Verily I say unto you, All these things shall come upon this generation. O Jerusalem, Jerusalem, thou that killest the prophets, and stonest them which are sent unto thee; how often would I have gathered thy children together, even as a hen gathereth her chickens under her wings, and ye would not! Behold, your house is left unto you desolate. For I say unto you, Ye shall not see Me henceforth, till ye shall say, Blessed is He that cometh in the Name of the Lord.

The Book of the Gospels.

¶ St. John the Evangelist's Day.

St. John xxi. 19.

JESUS said unto Peter, Follow Me. Then Peter, turning about, seeth the disciple whom Jesus loved following; which also leaned on His Breast at supper, and said, Lord, which is he that betrayeth Thee? Peter seeing him saith to Jesus, Lord, and what shall this man do? Jesus saith unto him, If I will that he tarry till I come, what is that to thee? Follow thou Me. Then went this saying abroad among the brethren, That that disciple should not die: yet Jesus said not unto him, He shall not die; but, If I will that he tarry till I come, what is that to thee? This is the disciple which testifieth of these things, and wrote these things, and we know that his testimony is true. And there are also many other things which Jesus did, the which if they should be written every one, I suppose that even the world itself could not contain the books that should be written.

¶ The Innocents' Day.

St. Matth. ii. 13.

THE Angel of the Lord appeareth to Joseph in a dream, saying, Arise, and take the Young Child, and His Mother, and flee into Egypt, and be thou there until I bring thee word; for Herod will seek the Young Child to destroy Him. When he arose, he took the Young Child and His Mother by night, and departed into Egypt, and was there until the death of Herod; that it

The Book of the Gospels.

might be fulfilled which was spoken of the Lord by the prophet, saying, Out of Egypt have I called My Son. Then Herod, when he saw that he was mocked of the Wise Men, was exceeding wroth; and sent forth, and slew all the children that were in Bethlehem, and in all the coasts thereof, from two years old and under, according to the time which he had diligently inquired of the Wise Men. Then was fulfilled that which was spoken by Jeremy the prophet, saying, In Rama was there a voice heard, lamentation, and weeping, and great mourning, Rachel weeping for her children, and would not be comforted, because they are not.

¶ The Sunday after Christmas-Day.

St. Matth. i. 18.

THE Birth of Jesus Christ was on this wise: When as His Mother Mary was espoused to Joseph, before they came together she was found with child of the Holy Ghost. Then Joseph her husband, being a just man, and not willing to make her a publick example, was minded to put her away privily. But while he thought on these things, behold, the Angel of the Lord appeared unto him in a dream, saying, Joseph thou son of David, fear not to take unto thee Mary thy wife; for That Which is conceived in her is of the Holy Ghost: And she shall bring forth a Son, and thou shalt call His Name JESUS; for He shall save His people from their sins. (Now all this was done, that it might be fulfilled which was spoken of the Lord by the prophet, saying, Behold, a Virgin shall be with child, and shall bring forth a Son, and they shall call His Name Emmanuel, which being interpreted is, God

The Book of the Gospels.

with us.) Then Joseph, being raised from sleep, did as the Angel of the Lord had bidden him, and took unto him his wife; and knew her not till she had brought forth her first-born Son: and he called His Name JESUS.

¶ The Circumcision of Christ.

St. Luke ii. 15.

AND it came to pass, as the Angels were gone away from them into heaven, the shepherds said one to another, Let us now go even unto Bethlehem, and see this thing which is come to pass, which the Lord hath made known unto us. And they came with haste, and found Mary and Joseph, and the Babe lying in a manger. And when they had seen it, they made known abroad the saying which was told them concerning this Child. And all they that heard it wondered at those things which were told them by the shepherds. But Mary kept all these things, and pondered them in her heart. And the shepherds returned, glorifying and praising God for all the things that they had heard and seen, as it was told unto them. And when eight days were accomplished for the circumcising of the Child, His Name was called JESUS, which was so named of the Angel before He was conceived in the womb.

¶ The same Collect, Epistle, and Gospel shall serve for every day after unto the Epiphany.

The Book of the Gospels.

❡ The Epiphany,

OR THE MANIFESTATION OF CHRIST TO THE GENTILES.

St. Matth. ii. 1.

WHEN Jesus was born in Bethlehem of Judæa, in the days of Herod the king, behold, there came Wise Men from the east to Jerusalem, saying, Where is He that is born King of the Jews? for we have seen His Star in the east, and are come to worship Him. When Herod the king had heard these things, he was troubled, and all Jerusalem with him. And when he had gathered all the chief priests and scribes of the people together, he demanded of them, where Christ should be born. And they said unto him, In Bethlehem of Judæa: for thus it is written by the prophet, And thou, Bethlehem, in the land of Juda, art not the least among the princes of Juda: for out of thee shall come a Governor that shall rule My people Israel. Then Herod, when he had privily called the Wise Men, enquired of them diligently what time the Star appeared. And he sent them to Bethlehem, and said, Go, and search diligently for the Young Child, and when ye have found Him, bring me word again, that I may come and worship Him also. When they had heard the king, they departed; and lo, the Star which they saw in the east went before them, till it came and stood over where the Young Child was. When they saw the Star, they rejoiced with exceeding great joy. And when they were come into the house, they saw the Young Child with Mary His Mother, and fell down and worshipped Him: and when they had opened their treasures, they presented unto Him gifts; gold, and frankincense, and myrrh. And being warned of God in a dream that they should not return to Herod, they departed into their own country another way.

The Book of the Gospels.

¶ The First Sunday after the Epiphany.

St. Luke ii. 41.

NOW His parents went to Jerusalem every year at the feast of the Passover. And when He was twelve years old, they went up to Jerusalem, after the custom of the feast. And when they had fulfilled the days, as they returned, the Child Jesus tarried behind in Jerusalem; and Joseph and His Mother knew not of it. But they, supposing Him to have been in the company, went a day's journey, and they sought Him among their kinsfolk and acquaintance. And when they found Him not, they turned back again to Jerusalem, seeking Him. And it came to pass, that after three days they found Him in the temple, sitting in the midst of the doctors, both hearing them, and asking them questions. And all that heard Him were astonished at His understanding and answers. And when they saw Him, they were amazed: and His Mother said unto Him, Son, why hast Thou thus dealt with us? behold, Thy father and I have sought Thee sorrowing. And He said unto them, How is it that ye sought Me? wist ye not that I must be about My Father's business? And they understood not the saying which He spake unto them. And He went down with them, and came to Nazareth, and was subject unto them: but His Mother kept all these sayings in her heart. And Jesus increased in wisdom, and stature, and in favour with God and man.

The Book of the Gospels.

¶ The Second Sunday after the Epiphany.

St. John ii. 1.

ND the third day there was a marriage in Cana of Galilee, and the Mother of Jesus was there. And both Jesus was called, and His disciples, to the marriage. And when they wanted wine, the Mother of Jesus saith unto Him, They have no wine. Jesus saith unto her, Woman, what have I to do with thee? Mine hour is not yet come. His Mother saith unto the servants, Whatsoever He saith unto you, do it. And there were set there six water-pots of stone, after the manner of the purifying of the Jews, containing two or three firkins apiece. Jesus saith unto them, Fill the water-pots with water. And they filled them up to the brim. And He saith unto them, Draw out now, and bear unto the governor of the feast. And they bare it. When the ruler of the feast had tasted the water that was made wine, and knew not whence it was, (but the servants which drew the water knew,) the governor of the feast called the bridegroom, and saith unto him, Every man at the beginning doth set forth good wine, and when men have well drunk, then that which is worse: but thou hast kept the good wine until now. This beginning of miracles did Jesus in Cana of Galilee, and manifested forth His glory, and His disciples believed on Him.

The Book of the Gospels.

¶ The Third Sunday after the Epiphany.

St. Matth. viii. 1.

WHEN He was come down from the mountain, great multitudes followed Him. And behold, there came a leper and worshipped Him, saying, Lord, if Thou wilt, Thou canst make me clean. And Jesus put forth His Hand, and touched him, saying, I will; be thou clean. And immediately his leprosy was cleansed. And Jesus saith unto him, See thou tell no man, but go thy way, shew thyself to the priest, and offer the gift that Moses commanded, for a testimony unto them. And when Jesus was entered into Capernaum, there came unto Him a centurion beseeching Him, and saying, Lord, my servant lieth at home sick of the palsy, grievously tormented. And Jesus saith unto him, I will come and heal him. The centurion answered and said, Lord, I am not worthy that Thou shouldest come under my roof; but speak the word only, and my servant shall be healed. For I am a man under authority, having soldiers under me: and I say unto this man, Go, and he goeth; and to another, Come, and he cometh; and to my servant, Do this, and he doeth it. When Jesus heard it, He marvelled, and said to them that followed, Verily I say unto you, I have not found so great faith, no not in Israel. And I say unto you, that many shall come from the east and west, and shall sit down with Abraham, and Isaac, and Jacob, in the kingdom of heaven. But the children of the kingdom shall be cast out into outer darkness: there shall be weeping and gnashing of teeth. And Jesus said unto the centurion, Go thy way, and as thou hast believed, so be it done unto thee. And his servant was healed in the selfsame hour.

The Book of the Gospels.

¶ The Fourth Sunday after the Epiphany.

St. Matth. viii. 23.

AND when He was entered into a ship, His disciples followed Him. And behold, there arose a great tempest in the sea, insomuch that the ship was covered with the waves: but He was asleep. And His disciples came to Him, and awoke Him, saying, Lord, save us, we perish. And He saith unto them, Why are ye fearful, O ye of little faith? Then He arose, and rebuked the winds and the sea, and there was a great calm. But the men marvelled, saying, What manner of man is this, that even the winds and the sea obey Him! And when He was come to the other side into the country of the Gergesenes, there met Him two possessed with devils, coming out of the tombs, exceeding fierce, so that no man might pass by that way. And behold, they cried out, saying, What have we to do with Thee, Jesus, Thou Son of God? art Thou come hither to torment us before the time? And there was a good way off from them an herd of many swine, feeding. So the devils besought Him, saying, If Thou cast us out, suffer us to go away into the herd of swine. And He said unto them, Go. And when they were come out, they went into the herd of swine: and behold, the whole herd of swine ran violently down a steep place into the sea, and perished in the waters. And they that kept them fled, and went their ways into the city, and told every thing, and what was befallen to the possessed of the devils. And behold, the whole city came out to meet Jesus: and when they saw Him, they besought Him, that He would depart out of their coasts.

The Book of the Gospels.

⁋ The Fifth Sunday after the Epiphany.

St. Matth. xiii. 24.

HE kingdom of heaven is likened unto a man which sowed good seed in his field. But while men slept, his enemy came and sowed tares among the wheat, and went his way. But when the blade was sprung up, and brought forth fruit, then appeared the tares also. So the servants of the housholder came, and said unto him, Sir, didst not thou sow good seed in thy field? from whence then hath it tares? He said unto them, An enemy hath done this. The servants said unto him, Wilt thou then that we go and gather them up? But he said, Nay; lest while ye gather up the tares, ye root up also the wheat with them. Let both grow together until the harvest; and in the time of harvest I will say to the reapers, Gather ye together first the tares, and bind them in bundles to burn them: but gather the wheat into my barn.

⁋ The Sixth Sunday after the Epiphany.

St. Matth. xxiv. 23.

HEN if any man shall say unto you, Lo, here is Christ, or there; believe it not. For there shall arise false Christs, and false prophets, and shall shew great signs and wonders; insomuch that (if it were possible) they shall deceive the very elect. Behold, I have told you before. Wherefore, if they shall say unto you, Behold, He is in the desert; go not forth: behold, He is in the secret chambers;

The Book of the Gospels.

believe it not. For as the lightning cometh out of the east, and shineth even unto the west; so shall also the coming of the Son of Man be. For wheresoever the carcase is, there will the eagles be gathered together. Immediately after the tribulation of those days shall the sun be darkened, and the moon shall not give her light, and the stars shall fall from heaven, and the powers of the heavens shall be shaken. And then shall appear the Sign of the Son of Man in heaven: and then shall all the tribes of the earth mourn, and they shall see the Son of Man coming in the clouds of heaven, with power and great glory. And He shall send His angels with a great sound of a trumpet, and they shall gather together His elect from the four winds, from one end of heaven to the other.

¶ The Sunday called Septuagesima,

OR THE THIRD SUNDAY BEFORE LENT.

St. Matth. xx. 1.

THE kingdom of heaven is like unto a man that is an householder, which went out early in the morning to hire labourers into his vineyard. And when he had agreed with the labourers for a penny a day, he sent them into his vineyard. And he went out about the third hour, and saw others standing idle in the market-place, and said unto them, Go ye also into the vineyard, and whatsoever is right I will give you. And they went their way. Again he went out about the sixth and ninth hour, and did likewise. And about the eleventh hour he went out, and found others standing idle, and saith unto them, Why stand ye here all the day idle? They say unto him, Because no man hath hired us. He saith unto them, Go ye also into the vineyard, and whatsoever is right,

The Book of the Gospels.

⁋ The Fifth Sunday after the Epiphany.

St. Matth. xiii. 24.

HE kingdom of heaven is likened unto a man which sowed good seed in his field. But while men slept, his enemy came and sowed tares among the wheat, and went his way. But when the blade was sprung up, and brought forth fruit, then appeared the tares also. So the servants of the housholder came, and said unto him, Sir, didst not thou sow good seed in thy field? from whence then hath it tares? He said unto them, An enemy hath done this. The servants said unto him, Wilt thou then that we go and gather them up? But he said, Nay; lest while ye gather up the tares, ye root up also the wheat with them. Let both grow together until the harvest; and in the time of harvest I will say to the reapers, Gather ye together first the tares, and bind them in bundles to burn them: but gather the wheat into my barn.

⁋ The Sixth Sunday after the Epiphany.

St. Matth. xxiv. 23.

HEN if any man shall say unto you, Lo, here is Christ, or there; believe it not. For there shall arise false Christs, and false prophets, and shall shew great signs and wonders; insomuch that (if it were possible) they shall deceive the very elect. Behold, I have told you before. Wherefore, if they shall say unto you, Behold, He is in the desert; go not forth: behold, He is in the secret chambers;

The Book of the Gospels.

believe it not. For as the lightning cometh out of the east, and shineth even unto the west; so shall also the coming of the Son of Man be. For wheresoever the carcase is, there will the eagles be gathered together. Immediately after the tribulation of those days shall the sun be darkened, and the moon shall not give her light, and the stars shall fall from heaven, and the powers of the heavens shall be shaken. And then shall appear the Sign of the Son of Man in heaven: and then shall all the tribes of the earth mourn, and they shall see the Son of Man coming in the clouds of heaven, with power and great glory. And He shall send His angels with a great sound of a trumpet, and they shall gather together His elect from the four winds, from one end of heaven to the other.

¶ The Sunday called Septuagesima,

OR THE THIRD SUNDAY BEFORE LENT.

St. Matth. xx. 1.

THE kingdom of heaven is like unto a man that is an housholder, which went out early in the morning to hire labourers into his vineyard. And when he had agreed with the labourers for a penny a day, he sent them into his vineyard. And he went out about the third hour, and saw others standing idle in the market-place, and said unto them, Go ye also into the vineyard, and whatsoever is right I will give you. And they went their way. Again he went out about the sixth and ninth hour, and did likewise. And about the eleventh hour he went out, and found others standing idle, and saith unto them, Why stand ye here all the day idle? They say unto him, Because no man hath hired us. He saith unto them, Go ye also into the vineyard, and whatsoever is right,

The Book of the Gospels.

that shall ye receive. So when even was come, the lord of the vineyard saith unto his steward, Call the labourers, and give them their hire, beginning from the last unto the first. And when they came that were hired about the eleventh hour, they received every man a penny. But when the first came, they supposed that they should have received more; and they likewise received every man a penny. And when they had received it, they murmured against the goodman of the house, saying, These last have wrought but one hour, and thou hast made them equal unto us, which have borne the burden and heat of the day. But he answered one of them, and said, Friend, I do thee no wrong; didst not thou agree with me for a penny? Take that thine is, and go thy way; I will give unto this last even as unto thee. Is it not lawful for me to do what I will with mine own? Is thine eye evil, because I am good? So the last shall be first, and the first last: for many be called, but few chosen.

¶ The Sunday called Sexagesima,

OR THE SECOND SUNDAY BEFORE LENT.

St. Luke viii. 4.

WHEN much people were gathered together, and were come to Him out of every city, He spake by a parable: A sower went out to sow his seed; and as he sowed, some fell by the way-side, and it was trodden down, and the fowls of the air devoured it. And some fell upon a rock, and as soon as it was sprung up, it withered away, because it lacked moisture. And some fell among thorns, and the thorns sprang up with it, and choked it. And other fell on good ground, and sprang up, and bare fruit an hundred-fold.

The Book of the Gospels.

And when He had said these things, He cried, He that hath ears to hear, let him hear. And His disciples asked Him, saying, What might this parable be? And He said, Unto you it is given to know the mysteries of the Kingdom of God: but to others in parables; that seeing they might not see, and hearing they might not understand. Now the parable is this: The seed is the Word of God. Those by the way-side are they that hear; then cometh the devil, and taketh away the word out of their hearts, lest they should believe, and be saved. They on the rock are they, which, when they hear, receive the word with joy; and these have no root, which for a while believe, and in time of temptation fall away. And that which fell among thorns, are they, which, when they have heard, go forth, and are choked with cares, and riches, and pleasures of this life, and bring no fruit to perfection. But that on the good ground, are they, which in an honest and good heart, having heard the word, keep it, and bring forth fruit with patience.

¶ The Sunday called Quinquagesima,

OR THE NEXT SUNDAY BEFORE LENT.

St. Luke xviii. 31.

THEN Jesus took unto Him the twelve, and said unto them, Behold, we go up to Jerusalem, and all things that are written by the prophets concerning the Son of Man shall be accomplished. For He shall be delivered unto the Gentiles, and shall be mocked, and spitefully entreated, and spitted on: and they shall scourge Him, and put Him to death; and the third day He shall rise again. And they understood none of these things: and this saying was hid from them, neither knew they the things which were spoken.

The Book of the Gospels.

And it came to pass, that as He was come nigh unto Jericho, a certain blind man sat by the way-side begging: and hearing the multitude pass by, he asked what it meant. And they told him, that Jesus of Nazareth passeth by. And he cried, saying, Jesus, Thou Son of David, have mercy on me. And they which went before rebuked him, that he should hold his peace: but he cried so much the more, Thou Son of David, have mercy on me. And Jesus stood, and commanded him to be brought unto Him: and when he was come near, He asked him, saying, What wilt thou that I should do unto thee? and he said, Lord, that I may receive my sight. And Jesus said unto him, Receive thy sight; thy faith hath saved thee. And immediately he received his sight, and followed Him, glorifying God: and all the people, when they saw it, gave praise unto God.

THE FIRST DAY OF LENT, COMMONLY CALLED
Ash Wednesday.

St. Matth. vi. 16.

WHEN ye fast, be not as the hypocrites, of a sad countenance: for they disfigure their faces, that they may appear unto men to fast. Verily I say unto you, They have their reward. But thou, when thou fastest, anoint thine head, and wash thy face, that thou appear not unto men to fast, but unto thy Father Which is in secret; and thy Father, Which seeth in secret, shall reward thee openly. Lay not up for yourselves treasures upon earth, where moth and rust doth corrupt, and where thieves break through and steal: but lay up for yourselves treasures in heaven, where neither moth nor rust doth corrupt, and where thieves do not break through nor steal: for where your treasure is, there will your heart be also.

The Book of the Gospels.

❧ The First Sunday in Lent.

St. Matth. iv. 1.

THEN was Jesus led up of the Spirit into the wilderness, to be tempted of the devil. And when He had fasted forty days and forty nights, He was afterward anhungred. And when the tempter came to Him, he said, If Thou be the Son of God, command that these stones be made bread. But He answered and said, It is written, Man shall not live by bread alone, but by every word that proceedeth out of the mouth of God. Then the devil taketh Him up into the holy city, and setteth Him on a pinnacle of the temple, and saith unto Him, If Thou be the Son of God, cast Thyself down; for it is written, He shall give His angels charge concerning Thee, and in their hands they shall bear Thee up, lest at any time Thou dash Thy foot against a stone. Jesus said unto him, It is written again, Thou shalt not tempt the Lord thy God. Again, the devil taketh Him up into an exceeding high mountain, and sheweth Him all the kingdoms of the world, and the glory of them; and saith unto Him, All these things will I give Thee, if Thou wilt fall down and worship me. Then saith Jesus unto him, Get thee hence, Satan; for it is written, Thou shalt worship the Lord thy God, and Him only shalt thou serve. Then the devil leaveth Him, and behold, angels came and ministered unto Him.

The Book of the Gospels.

❧ The Second Sunday in Lent.

St. Matth. xv. 21.

ESUS went thence, and departed into the coasts of Tyre and Sidon. And behold, a woman of Canaan came out of the same coasts, and cried unto Him, saying, Have mercy on me, O Lord, Thou Son of David; my daughter is grievously vexed with a devil. But He answered her not a word. And His disciples came and besought Him, saying, Send her away; for she crieth after us. But He answered and said, I am not sent, but unto the lost sheep of the House of Israel. Then came she and worshipped Him, saying, Lord, help me. But He answered and said, It is not meet to take the children's bread, and to cast it to dogs. And she said, Truth, Lord; yet the dogs eat of the crumbs which fall from their masters' table. Then Jesus answered and said unto her, O woman, great is thy faith: be it unto thee even as thou wilt. And her daughter was made whole from that very hour.

The Book of the Gospels.

¶ The Third Sunday in Lent.

St. Luke xi. 14.

JESUS was casting out a devil, and it was dumb. And it came to pass, when the devil was gone out, the dumb spake; and the people wondered. But some of them said, He casteth out devils through Beelzebub, the chief of the devils. And others, tempting Him, sought of Him a sign from heaven. But He, knowing their thoughts, said unto them, Every kingdom divided against itself is brought to desolation; and a house divided against a house falleth. If Satan also be divided against himself, how shall his kingdom stand? because ye say, that I cast out devils through Beelzebub. And if I by Beelzebub cast out devils, by whom do your sons cast them out? therefore shall they be your judges. But if I with the finger of God cast out devils, no doubt the kingdom of God is come upon you. When a strong man armed keepeth his palace, his goods are in peace; but when a stronger than he shall come upon him, and overcome him, he taketh from him all his armour wherein he trusted, and divideth his spoils. He that is not with Me is against Me: and he that gathereth not with Me, scattereth. When the unclean spirit is gone out of a man, he walketh through dry places, seeking rest; and finding none, he saith, I will return unto my house whence I came out. And when he cometh, he findeth it swept and garnished. Then goeth he and taketh to him seven other spirits more wicked than himself, and they enter in, and dwell there; and the last state of that man is worse than the first. And it came to pass, as He spake these things, a certain woman of the company lift up her voice, and said unto Him, Blessed is the Womb that bare Thee, and the paps which Thou hast sucked. But He said, Yea, rather, blessed are they that hear the Word of God, and keep it.

The Book of the Gospels.

⁋ The Fourth Sunday in Lent.

St. John vi. 1.

JESUS went over the sea of Galilee, which is the sea of Tiberias. And a great multitude followed Him, because they saw His miracles which He did on them that were diseased. And Jesus went up into a mountain, and there He sat with His disciples. And the Passover, a feast of the Jews, was nigh. When Jesus then lift up His eyes, and saw a great company come unto Him, He saith unto Philip, Whence shall we buy bread, that these may eat? (And this He said to prove him; for He Himself knew what He would do.) Philip answered Him, Two hundred penny-worth of bread is not sufficient for them, that every one of them may take a little. One of His disciples, Andrew, Simon Peter's brother, saith unto Him, There is a lad here, which hath five barley-loaves, and two small fishes: but what are they among so many? And Jesus said, Make the men sit down. Now there was much grass in the place. So the men sat down, in number about five thousand. And Jesus took the loaves, and when He had given thanks He distributed to the disciples, and the disciples to them that were set down; and likewise of the fishes as much as they would. When they were filled, He said unto His disciples, Gather up the fragments that remain, that nothing be lost. Therefore they gathered them together, and filled twelve baskets with the fragments of the five barley-loaves, which remained over and above unto them that had eaten. Then those men, when they had seen the miracle that Jesus did, said, This is of a truth that Prophet that should come into the world.

The Book of the Gospels.

¶ The Fifth Sunday in Lent.

[COMMONLY CALLED PASSION SUNDAY.]

St. John viii. 46.

JESUS said, Which of you convinceth Me of sin? and if I say the truth, why do ye not believe Me? He that is of God heareth God's words; ye therefore hear them not, because ye are not of God. Then answered the Jews, and said unto Him, Say we not well, that Thou art a Samaritan, and hast a devil? Jesus answered, I have not a devil; but I honour My Father, and ye do dishonour Me. And I seek not Mine Own glory; there is One that seeketh and judgeth. Verily, verily, I say unto you, If a man keep My saying, he shall never see death. Then said the Jews unto Him, Now we know that Thou hast a devil: Abraham is dead, and the prophets; and Thou sayest, If a man keep My saying, he shall never taste of death. Art Thou greater than our father Abraham, which is dead? and the prophets are dead: whom makest Thou Thyself? Jesus answered, If I honour Myself, My honour is nothing; it is My Father that honoureth Me, of Whom ye say, that He is your God: yet ye have not known Him; but I know Him: and if I should say, I know Him not, I shall be a liar like unto you; but I know Him, and keep His saying. Your father Abraham rejoiced to see My day, and he saw it, and was glad. Then said the Jews unto Him, Thou art not yet fifty years old, and hast Thou seen Abraham? Jesus said unto them, Verily, verily, I say unto you, Before Abraham was, I Am. Then took they up stones to cast at Him: but Jesus hid Himself, and went out of the temple.

The Book of the Gospels.

¶ The Sunday next before Easter.

[COMMONLY CALLED PALM SUNDAY.]

St. Matth. xxvii. 1.

HEN the morning was come, all the chief priests and elders of the people took counsel against Jesus, to put Him to death. And when they had bound Him, they led Him away, and delivered Him to Pontius Pilate the governour. Then Judas who had betrayed Him, when he saw that He was condemned, repented himself, and brought again the thirty pieces of silver to the chief priests and elders, saying, I have sinned, in that I have betrayed the innocent blood. And they said, What is that to us? see thou to that. And he cast down the pieces of silver in the temple, and departed, and went and hanged himself. And the chief priests took the silver pieces, and said, It is not lawful for to put them into the treasury, because it is the price of blood. And they took counsel, and bought with them the potter's field, to bury strangers in. Wherefore that field was called, The Field of Blood, unto this day. (Then was fulfilled that which was spoken by Jeremy the prophet, saying, And they took the thirty pieces of silver, the price of Him that was valued, Whom they of the children of Israel did value, and gave them for the potter's field, as the Lord appointed me.) And Jesus stood before the governour; and the governour asked Him, saying, Art Thou the King of the Jews? And Jesus said unto him, Thou sayest. And when He was accused of the chief priests and elders, He answered nothing. Then saith Pilate unto Him, Hearest Thou not how many things they witness against Thee? And He answered him to never a word, insomuch that the

The Book of the Gospels.

governour marvelled greatly. Now at that feast the governour was wont to release unto the people a prisoner, whom they would. And they had then a notable prisoner, called Barabbas. Therefore when they were gathered together, Pilate said unto them, Whom will ye that I release unto you? Barabbas, or Jesus which is called Christ? For he knew that for envy they had delivered Him. When he was set down on the judgment-seat, his wife sent unto him, saying, Have thou nothing to do with that just Man: for I have suffered many things this day in a dream because of Him. But the chief priests and elders persuaded the multitude that they should ask Barabbas, and destroy Jesus. The governour answered and said unto them, Whether of the twain will ye that I release unto you? They said, Barabbas. Pilate saith unto them, What shall I do then with Jesus, which is called Christ? They all say unto him, Let Him be crucified. And the governour said, Why, what evil hath He done? But they cried out the more, saying, Let Him be crucified. When Pilate saw that he could prevail nothing, but that rather a tumult was made, he took water, and washed his hands before the multitude, saying, I am innocent of the Blood of this just Person: see ye to it. Then answered all the people, and said, His Blood be on us, and on our children. Then released he Barabbas unto them: and when he had scourged Jesus he delivered Him to be crucified. Then the soldiers of the governour took Jesus into the common hall, and gathered unto Him the whole band of soldiers. And they stripped Him, and put on Him a scarlet robe. And when they had platted a Crown of Thorns they put it upon His Head, and a Reed in His Right Hand: and they bowed the knee before Him, and mocked Him, saying, Hail, King of the Jews. And they spit upon Him, and took the reed, and smote Him on the Head. And after that they had mocked Him they took the robe off from Him, and put His Own raiment on Him, and led Him away to crucify Him. And as they came out they found a man of Cyrene, Simon by name;

The Book of the Gospels.

him they compelled to bear His Cross. And when they were come unto a place called Golgotha, that is to say, a place of a scull, they gave Him vinegar to drink mingled with gall: and when He had tasted thereof, He would not drink. And they crucified Him, and parted His garments, casting lots: that it might be fulfilled, which was spoken by the prophet, They parted My garments among them, and upon My vesture did they cast lots. And sitting down they watched Him there; and set up over His Head His accusation written, THIS IS JESUS THE KING OF THE JEWS. Then were there two thieves crucified with Him; one on the right hand, and another on the left. And they that passed by reviled Him, wagging their heads, and saying, Thou that destroyest the temple, and buildest it in three days, save Thyself: if Thou be the Son of God, come down from the Cross. Likewise also the chief priests mocking Him, with the scribes and elders, said, He saved others, Himself He cannot save: if He be the King of Israel, let Him now come down from the Cross, and we will believe Him. He trusted in God; let Him deliver Him now, if He will have Him: for He said, I am the Son of God. The thieves also, which were crucified with Him, cast the same in His teeth. Now from the sixth hour there was darkness over all the land unto the ninth hour. And about the ninth hour Jesus cried with a loud voice, saying, *Eli, Eli, lama sabachthani?* that is to say, My God, My God, why hast Thou forsaken Me? Some of them that stood there, when they heard that, said, This man calleth for Elias. And straightway one of them ran, and took a spunge, and filled it with vinegar, and put it on a reed, and gave Him to drink. The rest said, Let be, let us see whether Elias will come to save Him. Jesus, when He had cried again with a loud voice, yielded up the ghost. And behold, the vail of the temple was rent in twain from the top to the bottom, and the earth did quake, and the rocks rent, and the graves were opened, and many bodies of saints which slept arose,

The Book of the Gospels.

and came out of the graves after His resurrection, and went into the holy city, and appeared unto many. Now when the centurion, and they that were with him, watching Jesus, saw the earthquake, and those things that were done, they feared greatly, saying, Truly this was the Son of God.

¶ The Monday before Easter.

St. Mark xiv. 1.

AFTER two days was the feast of the Passover, and of unleavened bread: and the chief priests and the scribes sought how they might take Him by craft, and put Him to death. But they said, Not on the feast-day, lest there be an uproar of the people. And being in Bethany, in the house of Simon the leper, as He sat at meat, there came a woman having an alabaster box of ointment of spikenard, very precious; and she brake the box, and poured it on His Head. And there were some that had indignation within themselves, and said, Why was this waste of the ointment made? for it might have been sold for more than three hundred pence, and have been given to the poor: and they murmured against her. And Jesus said, Let her alone; why trouble ye her? she hath wrought a good work on Me: for ye have the poor with you always, and whensoever ye will ye may do them good; but Me ye have not always. She hath done what she could; she is come aforehand to anoint My Body to the burying. Verily I say unto you, Wheresoever this Gospel shall be preached throughout the whole world, this also that she hath done shall be spoken of for a memorial of her. And Judas Iscariot, one of the twelve, went unto the chief priests to betray Him unto them. And when they heard it they were glad,

The Book of the Gospels.

and promised to give him money. And he sought how he might conveniently betray Him. And the first day of unleavened bread, when they killed the passover, His disciples said unto Him, Where wilt Thou that we go and prepare, that Thou mayest eat the passover? And He sendeth forth two of His disciples, and saith unto them, Go ye into the city, and there shall meet you a man bearing a pitcher of water; follow him: And wheresoever he shall go in, say ye to the good-man of the house, The Master saith, Where is the guest-chamber, where I shall eat the passover with My disciples? And he will shew you a large upper-room furnished, and prepared: there make ready for us. And His disciples went forth, and came into the city, and found as He had said unto them: and they made ready the passover. And in the evening He cometh with the twelve. And as they sat, and did eat, Jesus said, Verily I say unto you, One of you which eateth with Me shall betray Me. And they began to be sorrowful, and to say unto Him one by one, Is it I? and another said, Is it I? And He answered and said unto them, It is one of the twelve that dippeth with Me in the dish. The Son of Man indeed goeth, as it is written of Him: but woe to that man by whom the Son of Man is betrayed: good were it for that man if he had never been born. And as they did eat, Jesus took bread, and blessed, and brake it, and gave to them, and said, Take, eat: This is My Body. And He took the cup, and when He had given thanks He gave it to them: and they all drank of it. And He said unto them, This is My Blood of the new testament, which is shed for many. Verily I say unto you, I will drink no more of the fruit of the vine, until that day that I drink it new in the Kingdom of God. And when they had sung an hymn they went out into the mount of Olives. And Jesus saith unto them, All ye shall be offended because of Me this night: for it is written, I will smite the Shepherd, and the sheep shall be scattered. But, after that I am risen, I will go before you into Galilee. But Peter said unto

The Book of the Gospels.

Him, Although all shall be offended, yet will not I. And Jesus saith unto him, Verily I say unto thee, That this day, even in this night, before the cock crow twice, thou shalt deny Me thrice. But he spake the more vehemently, If I should die with Thee, I will not deny Thee in any wise. Likewise also said they all. And they came to a place which was named Gethsemane: and He saith to His disciples, Sit ye here, while I shall pray. And He taketh with Him Peter, and James, and John, and began to be sore amazed, and to be very heavy, and saith unto them, My Soul is exceeding sorrowful unto death; tarry ye here, and watch. And He went forward a little, and fell on the ground, and prayed, that, if it were possible, the hour might pass from Him. And He said, Abba, Father, all things are possible unto Thee; take away this cup from Me; nevertheless, not what I will, but what Thou wilt. And He cometh and findeth them sleeping, and saith unto Peter, Simon, sleepest thou? couldest not thou watch one hour? Watch ye and pray, lest ye enter into temptation: the spirit truly is ready, but the flesh is weak. And again He went away, and prayed, and spake the same words. And when He returned He found them asleep again, (for their eyes were heavy,) neither wist they what to answer Him. And He cometh the third time, and saith unto them, Sleep on now, and take your rest: it is enough, the hour is come; behold, the Son of Man is betrayed into the hands of sinners. Rise up, let us go; lo, he that betrayeth Me is at hand. And immediately, while He yet spake, cometh Judas, one of the twelve, and with him a great multitude with swords and staves, from the chief priests, and the scribes, and the elders. And he that betrayed Him had given them a token, saying, Whomsoever I shall kiss, that same is He; take Him, and lead Him away safely. And as soon as he was come, he goeth straightway to Him, and saith, Master, master; and kissed Him. And they laid their hands on Him, and took Him. And one of them that stood by drew a

The Book of the Gospels.

sword, and smote a servant of the high priest, and cut off his ear. And Jesus answered, and said unto them, Are ye come out as against a thief, with swords and with staves, to take Me? I was daily with you in the temple teaching, and ye took Me not: but the Scriptures must be fulfilled. And they all forsook Him, and fled. And there followed Him a certain young man, having a linen cloth cast about his naked body; and the young men laid hold on him: and he left the linen cloth, and fled from them naked. And they led Jesus away to the high priest: and with him were assembled all the chief priests, and the elders, and the scribes. And Peter followed Him afar off, even into the palace of the high priest; and he sat with the servants, and warmed himself at the fire. And the chief priests and all the council sought for witness against Jesus to put Him to death; and found none. For many bare false witness against Him, but their witness agreed not together. And there arose certain, and bare false witness against Him, saying, We heard Him say, I will destroy this temple that is made with hands, and within three days I will build another made without hands. But neither so did their witness agree together. And the high priest stood up in the midst, and asked Jesus, saying, Answerest Thou nothing? what is it which these witness against Thee? But He held His peace, and answered nothing. Again the high priest asked Him, and said unto Him, Art Thou the Christ, the Son of the Blessed? And Jesus said, I am; and ye shall see the Son of Man sitting on the right hand of power, and coming in the clouds of heaven. Then the high priest rent his clothes, and saith, What need we any further witnesses? ye have heard the blasphemy: what think ye? And they all condemned Him to be guilty of death. And some began to spit on Him, and to cover His Face, and to buffet Him, and to say unto Him, Prophesy: and the servants did strike Him with the palms of their hands. And as Peter was beneath in the palace there cometh one of the maids of the high priest; and when

The Book of the Gospels.

she saw Peter warming himself she looked upon him, and said, And thou also wast with Jesus of Nazareth. But he denied, saying, I know not, neither understand I what thou sayest. And he went out into the porch; and the cock crew. And a maid saw him again, and began to say to them that stood by, This is one of them. And he denied it again. And a little after, they that stood by said again to Peter, Surely thou art one of them; for thou art a Galilean, and thy speech agreeth thereto. But he began to curse and to swear, saying, I know not This Man of Whom ye speak. And the second time the cock crew. And Peter called to mind the word that Jesus said unto him, Before the cock crow twice, thou shalt deny Me thrice. And when he thought thereon, he wept.

⁋ The Tuesday before Easter.

St. Mark xv. 1.

AND straightway in the morning the chief priests held a consultation with the elders, and scribes, and the whole council, and bound Jesus, and carried Him away, and delivered Him to Pilate. And Pilate asked Him, Art Thou the King of the Jews? And He answering said unto him, Thou sayest it. And the chief priests accused Him of many things: but He answered nothing. And Pilate asked Him again, saying, Answerest Thou nothing? behold how many things they witness against Thee. But Jesus yet answered nothing: so that Pilate marvelled. Now at that feast he released unto them one prisoner, whomsoever they desired. And there was one named Barabbas, which lay bound with them that had made insurrection with him, who had committed murder in the insurrection.

The Book of the Gospels.

And the multitude, crying aloud, began to desire him to do as he had ever done unto them. But Pilate answered them, saying, Will ye that I release unto you the King of the Jews? For he knew that the chief priests had delivered Him for envy. But the chief priests moved the people, that he should rather release Barabbas unto them. And Pilate answered, and said again unto them, What will ye then that I shall do unto Him Whom ye call the King of the Jews? And they cried out again, Crucify Him. Then Pilate said unto them, Why, what evil hath He done? And they cried out the more exceedingly, Crucify Him. And so Pilate, willing to content the people, released Barabbas unto them, and delivered Jesus, when he had scourged Him, to be crucified. And the soldiers led Him away into the hall, called Prætorium; and they call together the whole band. And they clothed Him with purple, and platted a crown of thorns, and put it about His head: and began to salute Him, Hail, King of the Jews. And they smote Him on the head with a reed, and did spit upon Him, and bowing their knees worshipped Him. And when they had mocked Him they took off the purple from Him, and put His own clothes on Him, and led Him out to crucify Him. And they compel one Simon a Cyrenian, who passed by, coming out of the country, the father of Alexander and Rufus, to bear His Cross. And they bring Him unto the place Golgotha, which is, being interpreted, The place of a scull. And they gave Him to drink wine mingled with myrrh; but He received it not. And when they had crucified Him they parted His garments, casting lots upon them, what every man should take. And it was the third hour, and they crucified Him. And the superscription of His accusation was written over, THE KING OF THE JEWS. And with Him they crucify two thieves, the one on His right hand, and the other on His left. And the Scripture was fulfilled, which saith, And He was numbered with the transgressors. And they that passed by railed on Him, wagging their heads, and saying, Ah,

The Book of the Gospels.

Thou that destroyest the temple, and buildest it in three days, save Thyself, and come down from the cross. Likewise also the chief priests mocking said among themselves, with the scribes, He saved others; Himself He cannot save. Let Christ the King of Israel descend now from the cross, that we may see and believe. And they that were crucified with Him reviled Him. And when the sixth hour was come, there was darkness over the whole land until the ninth hour. And at the ninth hour Jesus cried with a loud voice, saying, *Eloi, Eloi, lama sabachthani?* which is, being interpreted, My God, My God, why hast Thou forsaken Me? And some of them that stood by, when they heard it, said, Behold, He calleth Elias. And one ran and filled a spunge full of vinegar, and put it on a reed, and gave Him to drink, saying, Let alone; let us see whether Elias will come to take Him down. And Jesus cried with a loud voice, and gave up the ghost. And the vail of the temple was rent in twain from the top to the bottom. And when the centurion, which stood over against Him, saw that He so cried out, and gave up the ghost, he said, Truly this Man was the Son of God.

¶ The Wednesday before Easter.

St. Luke xxii. 1.

NOW the feast of unleavened bread drew nigh, which is called the Passover. And the chief priests and scribes sought how they might kill Him; for they feared the people. Then entered Satan into Judas surnamed Iscariot, being of the number of the twelve. And he went his way, and communed with the chief priests and captains, how he might betray Him unto them. And they were glad, and covenanted to give him money. And he promised, and sought oppor-

The Book of the Gospels.

tunity to betray Him unto them in the absence of the multitude. Then came the day of unleavened bread, when the passover must be killed. And He sent Peter and John, saying, Go and prepare us the passover, that we may eat. And they said unto Him, Where wilt Thou that we prepare? And He said unto them, Behold, when ye are entered into the city, there shall a man meet you, bearing a pitcher of water; follow him into the house where he entereth in. And ye shall say unto the goodman of the house, The Master saith unto thee, Where is the guest-chamber, where I shall eat the passover with My disciples? And he shall shew you a large upper-room furnished; there make ready. And they went, and found as He had said unto them: and they made ready the passover. And when the hour was come He sat down, and the twelve Apostles with Him. And He said unto them, With desire I have desired to eat this passover with you before I suffer: for I say unto you, I will not any more eat thereof, until it be fulfilled in the Kingdom of God. And He took the cup, and gave thanks, and said, Take this, and divide it among yourselves. For I say unto you, I will not drink of the fruit of the vine, until the Kingdom of God shall come. And He took bread, and gave thanks, and brake it, and gave unto them, saying, This is My Body, which is given for you: this do in remembrance of Me. Likewise also the cup after supper, saying, This cup is the new testament in My Blood, which is shed for you. But behold, the hand of him that betrayeth Me is with Me on the table. And truly the Son of Man goeth as it was determined; but woe unto that man by whom He is betrayed. And they began to enquire among themselves, which of them it was that should do this thing. And there was also a strife among them, which of them should be accounted the greatest. And He said unto them, The kings of the Gentiles exercise lordship over them, and they that exercise authority upon them are called benefactors. But ye shall not be so: but he that is greatest among you, let him

The Book of the Gospels.

be as the younger; and he that is chief, as he that doth serve. For whether is greater, he that sitteth at meat, or he that serveth? is not he that sitteth at meat? but I am among you as he that serveth. Ye are they which have continued with Me in My temptations. And I appoint unto you a kingdom, as My Father hath appointed unto Me; that ye may eat and drink at My table in My kingdom, and sit on thrones, judging the twelve tribes of Israel. And the Lord said, Simon, Simon, behold, Satan hath desired to have you, that he may sift you as wheat: but I have prayed for thee, that thy faith fail not; and when thou art converted, strengthen thy brethren. And he said unto Him, Lord, I am ready to go with Thee both into prison and to death. And He said, I tell thee, Peter, the cock shall not crow this day, before that thou shalt thrice deny that thou knowest Me. And He said unto them, When I sent you without purse, and scrip, and shoes, lacked ye any thing? And they said, Nothing. Then said He unto them, But now, he that hath a purse, let him take it, and likewise his scrip: and he that hath no sword, let him sell his garment, and buy one. For I say unto you, That this that is written must yet be accomplished in Me, And He was reckoned among the transgressors: for the things concerning Me have an end. And they said, Lord, behold, here are two swords. And He said unto them, It is enough. And He came out, and went, as He was wont, to the mount of Olives, and His disciples also followed Him. And when He was at the place, He said unto them, Pray, that ye enter not into temptation. And He was withdrawn from them about a stone's cast, and kneeled down and prayed, saying, Father, if Thou be willing, remove this cup from Me: nevertheless, not My will, but Thine be done. And there appeared an angel unto Him from heaven, strengthening Him. And being in an agony He prayed more earnestly; and His sweat was as it were great drops of blood falling down to the ground. And when He rose up from prayer, and was come to His disciples, He found them sleeping

The Book of the Gospels.

for sorrow, and said unto them, Why sleep ye? rise and pray, lest ye enter into temptation. And while He yet spake, behold, a multitude, and he that was called Judas, one of the twelve, went before them, and drew near unto Jesus to kiss Him. But Jesus said unto him, Judas, betrayest thou the Son of Man with a kiss? When they who were about Him saw what would follow, they said unto Him, Lord, shall we smite with the sword? And one of them smote the servant of the high priest, and cut off his right ear. And Jesus answered and said, Suffer ye thus far. And He touched his ear, and healed him. Then Jesus said unto the chief priests, and captains of the temple, and the elders who were come to Him, Be ye come out as against a thief, with swords and staves? When I was daily with you in the temple, ye stretched forth no hands against Me: but this is your hour, and the power of darkness. Then took they Him, and led Him, and brought Him into the high priest's house: and Peter followed afar off. And when they had kindled a fire in the midst of the hall, and were set down together, Peter sat down among them. But a certain maid beheld him, as he sat by the fire, and earnestly looked upon him, and said, This man was also with Him. And he denied Him, saying, Woman, I know Him not. And after a little while another saw him, and said, Thou art also of them. And Peter said, Man, I am not. And about the space of one hour after, another confidently affirmed, saying, Of a truth this fellow also was with Him; for he is a Galilean. And Peter said, Man, I know not what thou sayest. And immediately, while he yet spake, the cock crew. And the Lord turned, and looked upon Peter; and Peter remembered the word of the Lord, how He had said unto him, Before the cock crow, thou shalt deny Me thrice. And Peter went out, and wept bitterly. And the men that held Jesus mocked Him, and smote Him. And when they had blindfolded Him, they struck Him on the face, and asked Him, saying, Prophesy, who is it that smote Thee? And many other things blasphemously spake they against Him. And as soon as it was day, the elders of the people, and the chief priests, and the scribes, came together, and led Him into their council, saying, Art Thou the Christ? tell us. And He said unto them, If I tell you, ye will not believe: and if I also ask you, ye will not answer Me, nor let Me go. Hereafter shall the Son of Man sit on the right hand of the power of God. Then said they all, Art Thou then the Son of God? And He said unto them, Ye say that I am. And they said, What need we any further witness? for we ourselves have heard of His own mouth.

¶ The Thursday before Easter.

[COMMONLY CALLED MAUNDY THURSDAY.]

St. Luke xxiii. 1.

HE whole multitude of them arose, and led Him unto Pilate. And they began to accuse Him, saying, We found this Fellow perverting the nation, and forbidding to give tribute to Cæsar, saying, That He Himself is Christ a King. And Pilate asked Him, saying, Art Thou the King of the Jews? And He answered him, and said, Thou sayest it. Then said Pilate to the chief priests, and to the people, I find no fault in This Man. And they were the more fierce, saying, He stirreth up the people, teaching throughout all Jewry, beginning from Galilee to this place. When Pilate heard of Galilee, he asked whether the Man were a Galilean. And as soon as he knew that He belonged unto Herod's jurisdiction, he sent Him to Herod, who himself was also at Jerusalem at that time. And when Herod saw Jesus he was exceeding glad; for he was desirous to see

The Book of the Gospels.

Him of a long season, because he had heard many things of Him; and he hoped to have seen some miracle done by Him. Then he questioned with Him in many words; but He answered him nothing. And the chief priests and scribes stood and vehemently accused Him. And Herod with his men of war set Him at nought, and mocked Him, and arrayed Him in a gorgeous robe, and sent Him again to Pilate. And the same day Pilate and Herod were made friends together; for before they were at enmity between themselves. And Pilate, when he had called together the chief priests, and the rulers, and the people, said unto them, Ye have brought This Man unto me, as one that perverteth the people: and behold, I, having examined Him before you, have found no fault in This Man touching those things whereof ye accuse Him: No, nor yet Herod: for I sent you to him; and lo, nothing worthy of death is done unto Him. I will therefore chastise Him, and release Him. For of necessity he must release one unto them at the feast. And they cried out all at once, saying, Away with This Man, and release unto us Barabbas: (who for a certain sedition made in the city, and for murder, was cast into prison.) Pilate therefore, willing to release Jesus, spake again to them. But they cried, saying, Crucify Him, crucify Him. And he said unto them the third time, Why, what evil hath He done? I have found no cause of death in Him: I will therefore chastise Him, and let Him go. And they were instant with loud voices, requiring that He might be crucified: and the voices of them and of the chief priests prevailed. And Pilate gave sentence that it should be as they required. And he released unto them him that for sedition and murder was cast into prison, whom they had desired; but he delivered Jesus to their will. And as they led Him away, they laid hold upon one Simon a Cyrenian, coming out of the country, and on him they laid the Cross, that he might bear it after Jesus. And there followed Him a great company of people, and of women, which also bewailed and lamented Him.

The Book of the Gospels.

But Jesus, turning unto them, said, Daughters of Jerusalem, weep not for Me, but weep for yourselves, and for your children. For behold, the days are coming, in the which they shall say, Blessed are the barren, and the wombs that never bare, and the paps which never gave suck. Then shall they begin to say to the mountains, Fall on us; and to the hills, Cover us. For if they do these things in a green tree, what shall be done in the dry? And there were also two other, malefactors, led with Him to be put to death. And when they were come to the place which is called Calvary, there they crucified Him; and the malefactors, one on the right hand, and the other on the left. Then said Jesus, Father, forgive them, for they know not what they do. And they parted His raiment, and cast lots. And the people stood beholding; and the rulers also with them derided Him, saying, He saved others; let Him save Himself, if He be Christ, the chosen of God. And the soldiers also mocked Him, coming to Him, and offering Him vinegar, and saying, If Thou be the King of the Jews, save Thyself. And a superscription also was written over Him in letters of Greek, and Latin, and Hebrew, THIS IS THE KING OF THE JEWS. And one of the malefactors, which were hanged, railed on Him, saying, If Thou be Christ, save Thyself, and us. But the other answering rebuked him, saying, Dost not thou fear God, seeing thou art in the same condemnation? And we indeed justly; for we receive the due reward of our deeds, but This Man hath done nothing amiss. And he said unto Jesus, Lord, remember me when Thou comest into Thy kingdom. And Jesus said unto him, Verily I say unto thee, To-day shalt thou be with Me in Paradise. And it was about the sixth hour: and there was a darkness over all the earth until the ninth hour. And the sun was darkened, and the vail of the temple was rent in the midst. And when Jesus had cried with a loud voice, He said, Father, into Thy hands I commend My Spirit: and having said thus, He gave up the ghost. Now when the centurion saw what

The Book of the Gospels.

was done, he glorified God, saying, Certainly This was a righteous Man. And all the people that came together to that sight, beholding the things that were done, smote their breasts, and returned. And all His acquaintance, and the women that followed Him from Galilee, stood afar off, beholding these things.

❡ Good Friday.

St. John xix. 1.

PILATE therefore took Jesus, and scourged Him. And the soldiers platted a Crown of Thorns, and put it on His Head, and they put on Him a Purple Robe, and said, Hail, King of the Jews: and they smote Him with their hands. Pilate therefore went forth again, and saith unto them, Behold, I bring Him forth to you, that ye may know that I find no fault in Him. Then came Jesus forth, wearing the crown of thorns, and the purple robe. And Pilate saith unto them, Behold the Man! When the chief priests therefore and officers saw Him, they cried out, saying, Crucify Him, crucify Him. Pilate saith unto them, Take ye Him, and crucify Him: for I find no fault in Him. The Jews answered him, We have a law, and by our law He ought to die, because He made Himself the Son of God. When Pilate therefore heard that saying, he was the more afraid; and went again into the judgment-hall, and saith unto Jesus, Whence art Thou? But Jesus gave him no answer. Then saith Pilate unto Him, Speakest Thou not unto me? knowest Thou not that I have power to crucify Thee, and have power to release Thee? Jesus answered, Thou couldest have no power at all against Me, except it were given thee from above: therefore he that delivered Me unto thee hath the greater sin. And from thenceforth Pilate sought to re-

The Book of the Gospels.

lease Him: but the Jews cried out, saying, If thou let this Man go, thou art not Cæsar's friend: whosoever maketh himself a king speaketh against Cæsar. When Pilate therefore heard that saying, he brought Jesus forth, and sat down in the judgment-seat, in a place that is called the Pavement, but in the Hebrew, Gabbatha. And it was the preparation of the passover, and about the sixth hour: and he saith unto the Jews, Behold your King! But they cried out, Away with Him, away with Him, crucify Him. Pilate saith unto them, Shall I crucify your King? The chief priests answered, We have no king but Cæsar. Then delivered he Him therefore unto them to be crucified: and they took Jesus, and led Him away. And He, bearing His Cross, went forth into a place called the Place of a Scull, which is called in the Hebrew, Golgotha: where they crucified Him, and two other with Him, on either side one, and Jesus in the midst. And Pilate wrote a title, and put it on the Cross; and the writing was, JESUS OF NAZARETH THE KING OF THE JEWS. This title then read many of the Jews: for the place where Jesus was crucified was nigh to the city: and it was written in Hebrew, and Greek, and Latin. Then said the chief priests of the Jews to Pilate, Write not, The King of the Jews; but that He said, I am the King of the Jews. Pilate answered, What I have written, I have written. Then the soldiers, when they had crucified Jesus, took His garments, and made four parts, to every soldier a part; and also His coat: now the coat was without seam, woven from the top throughout. They said therefore among themselves, Let us not rend it, but cast lots for it, whose it shall be: that the Scripture might be fulfilled, which saith, They parted My raiment among them, and for My vesture they did cast lots. These things therefore the soldiers did. Now there stood by the Cross of Jesus, His Mother, and His Mother's sister, Mary the wife of Cleophas, and Mary Magdalene. When Jesus therefore saw His Mother, and the disciple standing by, whom He loved, He saith unto His

The Book of the Gospels.

Mother, Woman, behold thy son. Then saith He to the disciple, Behold thy Mother. And from that hour that disciple took her unto his own home. After this, Jesus knowing that all things were now accomplished, that the Scripture might be fulfilled, saith, I thirst. Now there was set a vessel full of vinegar: and they filled a spunge with vinegar, and put it upon hyssop, and put it to His Mouth. When Jesus therefore had received the vinegar, He said, It is finished: and He bowed His Head, and gave up the ghost. The Jews therefore, because it was the preparation, that the bodies should not remain upon the cross on the sabbath-day, (for that sabbath-day was an high day,) besought Pilate that their legs might be broken, and that they might be taken away. Then came the soldiers, and brake the legs of the first, and of the other which was crucified with Him. But when they came to Jesus, and saw that He was dead already, they brake not His legs. But one of the soldiers with a spear pierced His Side, and forthwith came there out Blood and Water. And he that saw it bare record, and his record is true: and he knoweth that he saith true, that ye might believe. For these things were done that the Scripture should be fulfilled, A bone of Him shall not be broken. And again, another Scripture saith, They shall look on Him Whom they pierced.

The Book of the Gospels.

¶ Easter Even.

St. Matth. xxvii. 57.

HEN the even was come, there came a rich man of Arimathæa, named Joseph, who also himself was Jesus' disciple. He went to Pilate, and begged the Body of Jesus. Then Pilate commanded the Body to be delivered. And when Joseph had taken the Body, he wrapped It in a clean linen cloth, and laid It in his own new tomb, which he had hewn out in the rock; and he rolled a great stone to the door of the sepulchre, and departed. And there was Mary Magdalene, and the other Mary, sitting over against the sepulchre. Now the next day that followed the day of the preparation, the chief priests and Pharisees came together unto Pilate, saying, Sir, we remember that that deceiver said, while He was yet alive, After three days I will rise again. Command therefore that the sepulchre be made sure until the third day, lest His disciples come by night and steal Him away, and say unto the people, He is risen from the dead: so the last error shall be worse than the first. Pilate said unto them, Ye have a watch; go your way, make it as sure as ye can. So they went and made the sepulchre sure, sealing the stone, and setting a watch.

The Book of the Gospels.

☧ Easter Day.

St. John xx. 1.

HE first day of the week cometh Mary Magdalene early, when it was yet dark, unto the sepulchre, and seeth the stone taken away from the sepulchre. Then she runneth and cometh to Simon Peter, and to the other disciple whom Jesus loved, and saith unto them, They have taken away the Lord out of the sepulchre, and we know not where they have laid Him. Peter therefore went forth, and that other disciple, and came to the sepulchre. So they ran both together; and the other disciple did outrun Peter, and came first to the sepulchre; and he, stooping down and looking in, saw the linen clothes lying; yet went he not in. Then cometh Simon Peter following him, and went into the sepulchre, and seeth the linen clothes lie; and the napkin that was about His Head, not lying with the linen clothes, but wrapped together in a place by itself. Then went in also that other disciple which came first to the sepulchre, and he saw, and believed. For as yet they knew not the Scripture, that He must rise again from the dead. Then the disciples went away again unto their own home.

The Book of the Gospels.

¶ The Monday in Easter-Week.

St. Luke xxiv. 13.

BEHOLD, two of His disciples went that same day to a village called Emmaus, which was from Jerusalem about threescore furlongs. And they talked together of all these things which had happened. And it came to pass, that while they communed together, and reasoned, Jesus Himself drew near, and went with them. But their eyes were holden, that they should not know Him. And He said unto them, What manner of communications are these that ye have one to another, as ye walk, and are sad? And the one of them, whose name was Cleopas, answering, said unto Him, Art Thou only a stranger in Jerusalem, and hast not known the things which are come to pass there in these days? And He said unto them, What things? And they said unto Him, Concerning Jesus of Nazareth, Who was a prophet mighty in deed and word, before God and all the people: and how the chief priests and our rulers delivered Him to be condemned to death, and have crucified Him. But we trusted that it had been He Which should have redeemed Israel: and besides all this, to-day is the third day since these things were done. Yea, and certain women also of our company made us astonished, which were early at the sepulchre; and when they found not His Body, they came, saying, that they had also seen a Vision of Angels, which said that He was alive. And certain of them which were with us went to the sepulchre, and found it even so as the women had said; but Him they saw not. Then He said unto them, O fools, and slow of heart to believe all that the prophets have spoken: ought not Christ to have suffered these things, and to enter into His glory? And begin-

The Book of the Gospels.

ning at Moses, and all the prophets, He expounded unto them in all the Scriptures the things concerning Himself. And they drew nigh unto the village whither they went; and He made as though He would have gone further: but they constrained Him, saying, Abide with us, for it is towards evening, and the day is far spent. And He went in to tarry with them. And it came to pass, as He sat at meat with them, He took bread, and blessed it, and brake, and gave to them. And their eyes were opened, and they knew Him, and He vanished out of their sight. And they said one to another, Did not our heart burn within us, while He talked with us by the way, and while He opened to us the Scriptures? And they rose up the same hour, and returned to Jerusalem, and found the eleven gathered together, and them that were with them, saying, The Lord is risen indeed, and hath appeared to Simon. And they told what things were done in the way, and how He was known of them in breaking of bread.

¶ The Tuesday in Easter-Week.

St. Luke xxiv. 36.

JESUS Himself stood in the midst of them, and saith unto them, Peace be unto you. But they were terrified and affrighted, and supposed that they had seen a spirit. And He said unto them, Why are ye troubled, and why do thoughts arise in your hearts? Behold My Hands and My Feet, that it is I Myself: handle Me, and see; for a spirit hath not flesh and bones, as ye see Me have. And when He had thus spoken, He shewed them His Hands and His Feet. And while they yet believed not for joy, and wondered, He said unto them, Have ye here any meat? And they gave Him a

The Book of the Gospels.

piece of a broiled fish, and of an honey-comb. And He took it, and did eat before them. And He said unto them, These are the words which I spake unto you, while I was yet with you, that all things must be fulfilled which were written in the law of Moses, and in the Prophets, and in the Psalms concerning Me. Then opened He their understanding, that they might understand the Scriptures, and said unto them, Thus it is written, and thus it behoved Christ to suffer, and to rise from the dead the third day; and that repentance and remission of sins should be preached in His Name among all nations, beginning at Jerusalem. And ye are witnesses of these things.

¶ The First Sunday after Easter.

[COMMONLY CALLED LOW SUNDAY.]

St. John xx. 19.

THE same day at evening, being the first day of the week, when the doors were shut, where the disciples were assembled for fear of the Jews, came Jesus and stood in the midst, and saith unto them, Peace be unto you. And when He had so said, He shewed unto them His Hands and His Side. Then were the disciples glad when they saw the Lord. Then said Jesus to them again, Peace be unto you: As My Father hath sent Me, even so send I you. And when He had said this, He breathed on them, and saith unto them, Receive ye the Holy Ghost. Whosoever sins ye remit, they are remitted unto them; and whosoever sins ye retain, they are retained.

The Book of the Gospels.

¶ The Second Sunday after Easter.

St. John x. 11.

ESUS said, I am the Good Shepherd: the Good Shepherd giveth His life for the sheep. But he that is an hireling, and not the shepherd, whose own the sheep are not, seeth the wolf coming, and leaveth the sheep, and fleeth; and the wolf catcheth them, and scattereth the sheep. The hireling fleeth, because he is an hireling, and careth not for the sheep. I am the Good Shepherd, and know My sheep, and am known of Mine. As the Father knoweth Me, even so know I the Father: and I lay down My Life for the sheep. And other sheep I have, which are not of this fold; them also I must bring, and they shall hear My Voice; and there shall be One Fold, and One Shepherd.

¶ The Third Sunday after Easter.

St. John xvi. 16.

ESUS said to His disciples, A little while and ye shall not see Me; and again, a little while and ye shall see Me; because I go to the Father. Then said some of His disciples among themselves, What is this that He saith unto us, A little while and ye shall not see Me; and again, a little while and ye shall see Me; and, Because I go to the Father? They said therefore, What is this that He saith, A little while? we cannot tell what He saith. Now Jesus knew that they were desirous to ask Him, and said unto them,

The Book of the Gospels.

Do ye enquire among yourselves of that I said, A little while and ye shall not see Me; and again, a little while and ye shall see Me? Verily, verily I say unto you, That ye shall weep and lament, but the world shall rejoice: and ye shall be sorrowful, but your sorrow shall be turned into joy. A woman, when she is in travail, hath sorrow, because her hour is come: but as soon as she is delivered of the child, she remembereth no more the anguish, for joy that a man is born into the world. And ye now therefore have sorrow: but I will see you again, and your heart shall rejoice, and your joy no man taketh from you.

¶ The Fourth Sunday after Easter.

St. John xvi. 5.

JESUS said unto His disciples, Now I go My way to Him that sent Me, and none of you asketh Me, Whither goest Thou? But, because I have said these things unto you, sorrow hath filled your heart. Nevertheless, I tell you the truth; it is expedient for you that I go away: for if I go not away, the Comforter will not come unto you; but if I depart, I will send Him unto you. And when He is come, He will reprove the world of sin, and of righteousness, and of judgment: of sin, because they believe not on Me; of righteousness, because I go to My Father, and ye see Me no more; of judgment, because the prince of this world is judged. I have yet many things to say unto you, but ye cannot bear them now. Howbeit, when He, the Spirit of Truth, is come, He will guide you into all truth: for He shall not speak of Himself; but whatsoever He shall hear, that shall He speak: and He will shew you things to come. He shall glorify Me: for He

The Book of the Gospels.

shall receive of Mine, and shall shew it unto you. All things that the Father hath are Mine: therefore said I, that He shall take of Mine, and shall shew it unto you.

⁋ The Fifth Sunday after Easter.

St. John xvi. 23.

VERILY, verily I say unto you, Whatsoever ye shall ask the Father in My Name, He will give it you. Hitherto have ye asked nothing in My Name: ask, and ye shall receive, that your joy may be full. These things have I spoken unto you in proverbs: the time cometh when I shall no more speak unto you in proverbs, but I shall shew you plainly of the Father. At that day ye shall ask in My Name: and I say not unto you, that I will pray the Father for you; for the Father Himself loveth you, because ye have loved Me, and have believed that I came out from God. I came forth from the Father, and am come into the world: again, I leave the world, and go to the Father. His disciples said unto Him, Lo, now speakest Thou plainly, and speakest no proverb. Now are we sure that Thou knowest all things, and needest not that any man should ask Thee: by this we believe that Thou camest forth from God. Jesus answered them, Do ye now believe? Behold, the hour cometh, yea, is now come, that ye shall be scattered every man to his own, and shall leave Me alone: and yet I am not alone, because the Father is with Me. These things I have spoken unto you, that in Me ye might have peace. In the world ye shall have tribulation; but be of good cheer, I have overcome the world.

The Book of the Gospels.

❧ The Ascension-Day.

St. Mark xvi. 14.

JESUS appeared unto the eleven as they sat at meat, and upbraided them with their unbelief and hardness of heart, because they believed not them which had seen Him after He was risen. And He said unto them, Go ye into all the world, and preach the Gospel to every creature. He that believeth and is baptized shall be saved; but he that believeth not shall be damned. And these signs shall follow them that believe: In My Name shall they cast out devils; they shall speak with new tongues; they shall take up serpents; and if they drink any deadly thing, it shall not hurt them; they shall lay hands on the sick, and they shall recover. So then after the Lord had spoken unto them, He was received up into heaven, and sat on the right hand of God. And they went forth and preached every where, the Lord working with them, and confirming the Word with signs following.

The Book of the Gospels.

¶ The Sunday after Ascension-Day.

St. John xv. 26, *and part of Chapter* xvi.

HEN the Comforter is come, Whom I will send unto you from the Father, even the Spirit of Truth, Which proceedeth from the Father, He shall testify of Me. And ye also shall bear witness, because ye have been with Me from the beginning. These things have I spoken unto you, that ye should not be offended. They shall put you out of the synagogues: yea, the time cometh, that whosoever killeth you will think that he doeth God service. And these things will they do unto you, because they have not known the Father, nor Me. But these things have I told you, that, when the time shall come, ye may remember that I told you of them.

The Book of the Gospels.

¶ Whitsun=Day.

St. John xiv. 15.

JESUS said unto His disciples, If ye love Me, keep My commandments. And I will pray the Father, and He shall give you another Comforter, that He may abide with you for ever; even the Spirit of Truth, Whom the world cannot receive, because it seeth Him not, neither knoweth Him: but ye know Him; for He dwelleth with you, and shall be in you. I will not leave you comfortless; I will come to you. Yet a little while, and the world seeth Me no more; but ye see Me: because I live, ye shall live also. At that day ye shall know, that I am in My Father, and ye in Me, and I in you. He that hath My commandments, and keepeth them, he it is that loveth Me; and he that loveth Me shall be loved of My Father, and I will love him, and will manifest Myself to him. Judas saith unto Him, (not Iscariot,) Lord, how is it that Thou wilt manifest Thyself unto us, and not unto the world? Jesus answered and said unto him, If a man love Me, he will keep My words, and My Father will love him, and We will come unto him, and make Our abode with him. He that loveth Me not keepeth not My sayings: and the word which ye hear is not Mine, but the Father's Which sent Me. These things have I spoken unto you, being yet present with you. But the Comforter, Which is the Holy Ghost, Whom the Father will send in My Name, He shall teach you all things, and bring all things to your remembrance, whatsoever I have said unto you. Peace I leave with you, My peace I give unto you: not as the world giveth, give I unto

The Book of the Gospels.

you. Let not your heart be troubled, neither let it be afraid. Ye have heard how I said unto you, I go away, and come again unto you. If ye loved Me, ye would rejoice, because I said, I go unto the Father: for My Father is greater than I. And now I have told you before it come to pass, that, when it is come to pass, ye might believe. Hereafter I will not talk much with you: for the prince of this world cometh, and hath nothing in Me. But that the world may know that I love the Father; and as the Father gave Me commandment, even so I do.

¶ The Monday in Whitsun-Week.

St. John iii. 16.

OD so loved the world, that He gave His Only-begotten Son, that whosoever believeth in Him should not perish, but have everlasting life. For God sent not His Son into the world to condemn the world, but that the world through Him might be saved. He that believeth on Him is not condemned: but he that believeth not is condemned already; because he hath not believed in the Name of the Only-begotten Son of God. And this is the condemnation, that light is come into the world, and men loved darkness rather than light, because their deeds were evil. For every one that doeth evil hateth the light, neither cometh to the light, lest his deeds should be reproved. But he that doeth truth cometh to the light, that his deeds may be made manifest, that they are wrought in God.

The Book of the Gospels.

¶ The Tuesday in Whitsun-Week.

St. John x. 1.

ERILY, verily I say unto you, He that entereth not by the door into the sheepfold, but climbeth up some other way, the same is a thief and a robber. But he that entereth in by the door is the shepherd of the sheep: to him the porter openeth; and the sheep hear his voice, and he calleth his own sheep by name, and leadeth them out. And, when he putteth forth his own sheep, he goeth before them, and the sheep follow him; for they know his voice. And a stranger will they not follow; but will flee from him; for they know not the voice of strangers. This parable spake Jesus unto them: but they understood not what things they were which He spake unto them. Then said Jesus unto them again; Verily, verily I say unto you, I am the door of the sheep. All that ever came before Me are thieves and robbers; but the sheep did not hear them. I am the door; by Me if any man enter in, he shall be saved, and shall go in and out, and find pasture. The thief cometh not but for to steal, and to kill, and to destroy: I am come that they might have life, and that they might have it more abundantly.

The Book of the Gospels.

¶ Trinity Sunday.

St. John iii. 1.

HERE was a man of the Pharisees, named Nicodemus, a ruler of the Jews: the same came to Jesus by night, and said unto Him, Rabbi, we know that Thou art a teacher come from God: for no man can do these miracles that Thou doest, except God be with him. Jesus answered and said unto him, Verily, verily I say unto thee, Except a man be born again, he cannot see the Kingdom of God. Nicodemus saith unto Him, How can a man be born when he is old? can he enter the second time into his mother's womb, and be born? Jesus answered, Verily, verily I say unto thee, Except a man be born of water, and of the Spirit, he cannot enter into the Kingdom of God. That which is born of the flesh is flesh; and that which is born of the Spirit is spirit. Marvel not that I said unto thee, Ye must be born again. The wind bloweth where it listeth, and thou hearest the sound thereof, but canst not tell whence it cometh, and whither it goeth; so is every one that is born of the Spirit. Nicodemus answered and said unto Him, How can these things be? Jesus answered and said unto him, Art thou a master of Israel, and knowest not these things? Verily, verily I say unto thee, We speak that We do know, and testify that We have seen; and ye receive not Our witness. If I have told you earthly things, and ye believe not; how shall ye believe, if I tell you of heavenly things? And no man hath ascended up to heaven, but He that came down from heaven, even the Son of man, Who is in heaven. And as Moses lifted up the serpent in the wilderness, even so must the Son of Man be lifted up: that whosoever believeth in Him should not perish, but have eternal life.

The Book of the Gospels.

¶ The First Sunday after Trinity.

St. Luke xvi. 19.

THERE was a certain rich man, which was clothed in purple, and fine linen, and fared sumptuously every day. And there was a certain beggar named Lazarus, which was laid at his gate full of sores, and desiring to be fed with the crumbs, which fell from the rich man's table: moreover, the dogs came and licked his sores. And it came to pass, that the beggar died, and was carried by the angels into Abraham's bosom. The rich man also died, and was buried: and in hell he lift up his eyes being in torments, and seeth Abraham afar off, and Lazarus in his bosom. And he cried and said, Father Abraham, have mercy on me, and send Lazarus, that he may dip the tip of his finger in water, and cool my tongue; for I am tormented in this flame. But Abraham said, Son, remember that thou in thy life-time receivedst thy good things, and likewise Lazarus evil things; but now he is comforted, and thou art tormented. And besides all this, between us and you there is a great gulf fixed: so that they who would pass from hence to you cannot; neither can they pass to us, that would come from thence. Then he said, I pray thee therefore, father, that thou wouldest send him to my father's house: for I have five brethren; that he may testify unto them, lest they also come into this place of torment. Abraham saith unto him, They have Moses and the Prophets; let them hear them. And he said, Nay, father Abraham; but if one went unto them from the dead, they will repent. And he said unto him, If they hear not Moses and the prophets, neither will they be persuaded, though one rose from the dead.

The Book of the Gospels.

❦ The Second Sunday after Trinity.

St. Luke xiv. 16.

A CERTAIN man made a great supper, and bade many; and sent his servant at supper-time to say to them that were bidden, Come, for all things are now ready. And they all with one consent began to make excuse. The first said unto him, I have bought a piece of ground, and I must needs go and see it; I pray thee have me excused. And another said, I have bought five yoke of oxen, and I go to prove them; I pray thee have me excused. And another said, I have married a wife, and therefore I cannot come. So that servant came and shewed his lord these things. Then the master of the house being angry said to his servant, Go out quickly into the streets and lanes of the city, and bring in hither the poor, and the maimed, and the halt, and the blind. And the servant said, Lord, it is done as thou hast commanded, and yet there is room. And the lord said unto the servant, Go out into the highways and hedges, and compel them to come in, that my house may be filled. For I say unto you, That none of those men which were bidden shall taste of my supper.

The Book of the Gospels.

¶ The Third Sunday after Trinity.

St. Luke xv. 1.

HEN drew near unto Him all the publicans and sinners for to hear Him. And the Pharisees and Scribes murmured, saying, This Man receiveth sinners, and eateth with them. And He spake this parable unto them, saying, What man of you having an hundred sheep, if he lose one of them, doth not leave the ninety and nine in the wilderness, and go after that which is lost, until he find it? And when he hath found it, he layeth it on his shoulders, rejoicing. And when he cometh home, he calleth together his friends and neighbours, saying unto them, Rejoice with me, for I have found my sheep which was lost. I say unto you, That likewise joy shall be in heaven over one sinner that repenteth, more than over ninety and nine just persons, which need no repentance. Either what woman having ten pieces of silver, if she lose one piece, doth not light a candle, and sweep the house, and seek diligently till she find it? And when she hath found it, she calleth her friends and her neighbours together, saying, Rejoice with me, for I have found the piece which I had lost. Likewise, I say unto you, There is joy in the presence of the angels of God over one sinner that repenteth.

The Book of the Gospels.

❡ The Fourth Sunday after Trinity.

St. Luke vi. 36.

BE ye therefore merciful, as your Father also is merciful. Judge not, and ye shall not be judged: condemn not, and ye shall not be condemned: forgive, and ye shall be forgiven: give, and it shall be given unto you; good measure, pressed down, and shaken together, and running over, shall men give into your bosom. For with the same measure that ye mete withal, it shall be measured to you again. And He spake a parable unto them, Can the blind lead the blind? shall they not both fall into the ditch? The disciple is not above his master; but every one that is perfect shall be as his master. And why beholdest thou the mote that is in thy brother's eye, but perceivest not the beam that is in thine own eye? Either how canst thou say to thy brother, Brother, let me pull out the mote that is in thine eye, when thou thyself beholdest not the beam that is in thine own eye? Thou hypocrite, cast out first the beam out of thine own eye, and then shalt thou see clearly to pull out the mote that is in thy brother's eye.

The Book of the Gospels.

¶ The Fifth Sunday after Trinity.

St. Luke v. 1.

IT came to pass, that as the people pressed upon Him to hear the Word of God, He stood by the lake of Gennesareth, and saw two ships standing by the lake; but the fishermen were gone out of them, and were washing their nets. And He entered into one of the ships, which was Simon's, and prayed him that he would thrust out a little from the land: and He sat down, and taught the people out of the ship. Now when He had left speaking, He said unto Simon, Launch out into the deep, and let down your nets for a draught. And Simon answering said unto Him, Master, we have toiled all the night, and have taken nothing; nevertheless, at Thy word I will let down the net. And when they had done this, they inclosed a great multitude of fishes, and their net brake. And they beckoned unto their partners which were in the other ship, that they should come and help them. And they came, and filled both the ships, so that they began to sink. When Simon Peter saw it, he fell down at Jesus' knees, saying, Depart from me, for I am a sinful man, O Lord. For he was astonished, and all that were with him, at the draught of the fishes which they had taken; and so was also James, and John, the sons of Zebedee, which were partners with Simon. And Jesus said unto Simon, Fear not, from henceforth thou shalt catch men. And when they had brought their ships to land, they forsook all, and followed Him.

The Book of the Gospels.

❧ The Sixth Sunday after Trinity.

St. Matth. v. 20.

JESUS said unto His disciples, Except your righteousness shall exceed the righteousness of the Scribes and Pharisees, ye shall in no case enter into the Kingdom of Heaven. Ye have heard that it was said by them of old time, Thou shalt not kill: and whosoever shall kill, shall be in danger of the judgment. But I say unto you, that whosoever is angry with his brother without a cause shall be in danger of the judgment: and whosoever shall say to his brother, Raca, shall be in danger of the council: but whosoever shall say, Thou fool, shall be in danger of hell-fire. Therefore if thou bring thy gift to the altar, and there rememberest that thy brother hath ought against thee; leave there thy gift before the altar, and go thy way, first be reconciled to thy brother, and then come and offer thy gift. Agree with thine adversary quickly, whiles thou art in the way with him; lest at any time the adversary deliver thee to the judge, and the judge deliver thee to the officer, and thou be cast into prison. Verily I say unto thee, Thou shalt by no means come out thence, till thou hast paid the uttermost farthing.

The Book of the Gospels.

¶ The Seventh Sunday after Trinity.

St. Mark viii. 1.

N those days the multitude being very great, and having nothing to eat, Jesus called His disciples unto Him, and saith unto them, I have compassion on the multitude, because they have now been with Me three days, and have nothing to eat: and if I send them away fasting to their own houses, they will faint by the way; for divers of them came from far. And His disciples answered Him, From whence can a man satisfy these men with bread here in the wilderness? And He asked them, How many loaves have ye? And they said, Seven. And He commanded the people to sit down on the ground. And He took the seven loaves, and gave thanks, and brake, and gave to His disciples to set before them; and they did set them before the people. And they had a few small fishes; and He blessed, and commanded to set them also before them. So they did eat, and were filled: and they took up of the broken meat that was left seven baskets. And they that had eaten were about four thousand. And He sent them away.

The Book of the Gospels.

⁋ The Eighth Sunday after Trinity.

St. Matth. vii. 15.

EWARE of false prophets, which come to you in sheep's clothing, but inwardly they are ravening wolves. Ye shall know them by their fruits: do men gather grapes of thorns, or figs of thistles? Even so every good tree bringeth forth good fruit; but a corrupt tree bringeth forth evil fruit. A good tree cannot bring forth evil fruit; neither can a corrupt tree bring forth good fruit. Every tree that bringeth not forth good fruit is hewn down, and cast into the fire. Wherefore by their fruits ye shall know them. Not every one that saith unto Me, Lord, Lord, shall enter into the Kingdom of Heaven; but he that doeth the Will of My Father Which is in heaven.

⁋ The Ninth Sunday after Trinity.

St. Luke xvi. 1.

ESUS said unto His disciples, There was a certain rich man which had a steward; and the same was accused unto him that he had wasted his goods. And he called him, and said unto him, How is it that I hear this of thee? Give an account of thy stewardship; for thou mayest be no longer steward. Then the steward said within himself, What shall I do? for my lord taketh away from me the stewardship: I cannot dig, to beg I am ashamed. I am resolved what to do, that,

The Book of the Gospels.

when I am put out of the stewardship, they may receive me into their houses. So he called every one of his lord's debtors unto him, and said unto the first, How much owest thou unto my lord? And he said, An hundred measures of oil. And he said unto him, Take thy bill, and sit down quickly, and write fifty. Then said he to another, And how much owest thou? And he said, An hundred measures of wheat. And he said unto him, Take thy bill, and write fourscore. And the lord commended the unjust steward, because he had done wisely: for the children of this world are in their generation wiser than the children of light. And I say unto you, Make to yourselves friends of the mammon of unrighteousness; that when ye fail, they may receive you into everlasting habitations.

¶ The Tenth Sunday after Trinity.

St. Luke xix. 41.

AND when He was come near, He beheld the city, and wept over it, saying, If thou hadst known, even thou, at least in this thy day, the things which belong unto thy peace! but now they are hid from thine eyes. For the days shall come upon thee, that thine enemies shall cast a trench about thee, and compass thee round, and keep thee in on every side, and shall lay thee even with the ground, and thy children within thee; and they shall not leave in thee one stone upon another; because thou knewest not the time of thy visitation. And He went into the Temple, and began to cast out them that sold therein, and them that bought, saying unto them, It is written, My house is the house of prayer: but ye have made it a den of thieves. And He taught daily in the Temple.

The Book of the Gospels.

¶ The Eleventh Sunday after Trinity.

St. Luke xviii. 9.

JESUS spake this parable unto certain which trusted in themselves that they were righteous, and despised others: Two men went up into the Temple to pray; the one a Pharisee, and the other a Publican. The Pharisee stood and prayed thus with himself, God, I thank Thee, that I am not as other men are, extortioners, unjust, adulterers, or even as this Publican: I fast twice in the week, I give tithes of all that I possess. And the Publican, standing afar off, would not lift up so much as his eyes unto heaven, but smote upon his breast, saying, God be merciful to me a sinner. I tell you, this man went down to his house justified rather than the other: for every one that exalteth himself shall be abased; and he that humbleth himself shall be exalted.

¶ The Twelfth Sunday after Trinity.

St. Mark vii. 31.

JESUS, departing from the coasts of Tyre and Sidon, came unto the sea of Galilee, through the midst of the coasts of Decapolis. And they bring unto Him one that was deaf, and had an impediment in his speech; and they beseech Him to put His hand upon him. And He took him aside from the multitude, and put His fingers into his ears, and He spit, and touched his tongue; and looking up to hea-

The Book of the Gospels.

ven, He sighed, and saith unto him, *Ephphatha*, that is, Be opened. And straightway his ears were opened, and the string of his tongue was loosed, and he spake plain. And He charged them that they should tell no man: but the more He charged them, so much the more a great deal they published it; and were beyond measure astonished, saying, He hath done all things well; He maketh both the deaf to hear, and the dumb to speak.

¶ The Thirteenth Sunday after Trinity.

St. Luke x. 23.

BLESSED are the eyes which see the things that ye see. For I tell you, That many prophets and kings have desired to see those things which ye see, and have not seen them; and to hear those things which ye hear, and have not heard them. And behold, a certain Lawyer stood up, and tempted Him, saying, Master, what shall I do to inherit eternal life? He said unto him, What is written in the Law? how readest thou? And he answering said, Thou shalt love the Lord thy God with all thy heart, and with all thy soul, and with all thy strength, and with all thy mind; and thy neighbour as thyself. And He said unto him, Thou hast answered right; this do, and thou shalt live. But he, willing to justify himself, said unto Jesus, And who is my neighbour? And Jesus answering said, A certain man went down from Jerusalem to Jericho, and fell among thieves, which stripped him of his raiment, and wounded him, and departed, leaving him half dead. And by chance there came down a certain priest that way, and, when he saw him, he passed by on the other side. And likewise a Levite, when he was at the place, came and looked on him, and passed by

The Book of the Gospels.

on the other side. But a certain Samaritan, as he journeyed, came where he was; and, when he saw him, he had compassion on him, and went to him, and bound up his wounds, pouring in oil and wine, and set him on his own beast, and brought him to an inn, and took care of him. And on the morrow, when he departed, he took out two pence, and gave them to the host, and said unto him, Take care of him; and whatsoever thou spendest more, when I come again, I will repay thee. Which now of these three, thinkest thou, was neighbour unto him that fell among the thieves? And he said, He that shewed mercy on him. Then said Jesus unto him, Go, and do thou likewise.

¶ The Fourteenth Sunday after Trinity.

St. Luke xvii. 11.

AND it came to pass, as Jesus went to Jerusalem, that He passed through the midst of Samaria, and Galilee. And as He entered into a certain village, there met him ten men that were lepers, which stood afar off. And they lifted up their voices, and said, Jesus, Master, have mercy on us. And when He saw them, He said unto them, Go, shew yourselves unto the priests. And it came to pass, that, as they went, they were cleansed. And one of them, when he saw that he was healed, turned back, and with a loud voice glorified God, and fell down on his face at His feet, giving Him thanks; and he was a Samaritan. And Jesus answering said, Were there not ten cleansed? but where are the nine? There are not found that returned to give glory to God, save this stranger. And He said unto him, Arise, go thy way, thy faith hath made thee whole.

The Book of the Gospels.

¶ The Fifteenth Sunday after Trinity.

St. Matth. vi. 24.

NO man can serve two masters: for either he will hate the one, and love the other; or else he will hold to the one, and despise the other. Ye cannot serve God and Mammon. Therefore I say unto you, Take no thought for your life, what ye shall eat, or what ye shall drink; nor yet for your body, what ye shall put on: Is not the life more than meat, and the body than raiment? Behold the fowls of the air; for they sow not, neither do they reap, nor gather into barns; yet your heavenly Father feedeth them. Are ye not much better than they? Which of you by taking thought can add one cubit unto his stature? And why take ye thought for raiment? Consider the lilies of the field how they grow: they toil not, neither do they spin: and yet I say unto you, That even Solomon in all his glory was not arrayed like one of these. Wherefore, if God so clothe the grass of the field, which to-day is, and to-morrow is cast into the oven; shall He not much more clothe you, O ye of little faith? Therefore take no thought, saying, What shall we eat? or what shall we drink? or wherewithal shall we be clothed? (for after all these things do the Gentiles seek:) for your Heavenly Father knoweth that ye have need of all these things. But seek ye first the kingdom of God, and His righteousness, and all these things shall be added unto you. Take therefore no thought for the morrow; for the morrow shall take thought for the things of itself: sufficient unto the day is the evil thereof.

The Book of the Gospels.

¶ The Sixteenth Sunday after Trinity.

St. Luke vii. 11.

ND it came to pass the day after, that Jesus went into a city called Nain; and many of His disciples went with Him, and much people. Now when He came nigh to the gate of the city, behold, there was a dead man carried out, the only son of his mother, and she was a widow; and much people of the city was with her. And when the Lord saw her, He had compassion on her, and said unto her, Weep not. And He came and touched the bier, (and they that bare him stood still,) and He said, Young man, I say unto thee, Arise. And he that was dead sat up, and began to speak: and He delivered him to his mother. And there came a fear on all, and they glorified God, saying, That a great Prophet is risen up among us, and that God hath visited His people. And this rumour of Him went forth throughout all Judæa, and throughout all the region round about.

¶ The Seventeenth Sunday after Trinity.

St. Luke xiv. 1.

T came to pass, as Jesus went into the house of one of the chief Pharisees to eat bread on the sabbath-day, that they watched Him. And behold, there was a certain man before Him which had the dropsy. And Jesus answering spake unto the Lawyers and Pharisees, saying, Is it lawful to heal on the sabbath-day? And they held their peace. And He took him, and

The Book of the Gospels.

healed him, and let him go; and answered them, saying, Which of you shall have an ass, or an ox, fallen into a pit, and will not straightway pull him out on the sabbath-day? And they could not answer Him again to these things. And He put forth a parable to those which were bidden, when He marked how they chose out the chief rooms, saying unto them, When thou art bidden of any man to a wedding, sit not down in the highest room; lest a more honourable man than thou be bidden of him: and he that bade thee and him come and say to thee, Give this man place; and thou begin with shame to take the lowest room. But when thou art bidden, go and sit down in the lowest room; that, when he that bade thee cometh, he may say unto thee, Friend, go up higher: then shalt thou have worship in the presence of them that sit at meat with thee. For whosoever exalteth himself shall be abased; and he that humbleth himself shall be exalted.

¶ The Eighteenth Sunday after Trinity.

St. Matth. xxii. 34.

WHEN the Pharisees had heard that Jesus had put the Sadducees to silence, they were gathered together. Then one of them, who was a Lawyer, asked Him a question, tempting Him, and saying, Master, which is the great commandment in the Law? Jesus said unto him, Thou shalt love the Lord thy God with all thy heart, and with all thy soul, and with all thy mind. This is the first and great commandment. And the second is like unto it, Thou shalt love thy neighbour as thyself. On these two commandments hang all the Law and the Prophets. While the Pharisees

The Book of the Gospels.

were gathered together, Jesus asked them, saying, What think ye of Christ? whose Son is He? They say unto Him, The Son of David. He saith unto them, How then doth David in Spirit call Him Lord, saying, The Lord said unto my Lord, Sit Thou on My right hand, till I make Thine enemies Thy foot-stool? If David then call Him Lord, how is He his Son? And no man was able to answer Him a word; neither durst any man from that day forth ask Him any more questions.

¶ The Nineteenth Sunday after Trinity.

St. Matth. ix. 1.

JESUS entered into a ship, and passed over, and came into His own city. And behold, they brought to Him a man sick of the palsy, lying on a bed. And Jesus, seeing their faith, said unto the sick of the palsy, Son, be of good cheer, thy sins be forgiven thee. And behold, certain of the scribes said within themselves, This Man blasphemeth. And Jesus, knowing their thoughts, said, Wherefore think ye evil in your hearts? For whether is easier to say, Thy sins be forgiven thee? or to say, Arise, and walk? But that ye may know that the Son of Man hath power on earth to forgive sins, (then saith He to the sick of the palsy,) Arise, take up thy bed, and go unto thine house. And he arose, and departed to his house. But when the multitude saw it, they marvelled, and glorified God, Who had given such power unto men.

The Book of the Gospels.

¶ The Twentieth Sunday after Trinity.

St. Matth. xxii. 1.

ESUS said, The Kingdom of heaven is like unto a certain king, who made a marriage for his son; and sent forth his servants to call them that were bidden to the wedding; and they would not come. Again, he sent forth other servants, saying, Tell them which are bidden, Behold, I have prepared my dinner; my oxen and my fatlings are killed, and all things are ready; come unto the marriage. But they made light of it, and went their ways, one to his farm, another to his merchandise: and the remnant took his servants, and entreated them spitefully, and slew them. But when the king heard thereof, he was wroth; and he sent forth his armies, and destroyed those murderers, and burnt up their city. Then saith he to his servants, The wedding is ready, but they who were bidden were not worthy. Go ye therefore into the high-ways, and as many as ye shall find bid to the marriage. So those servants went out into the high-ways, and gathered together all, as many as they found, both bad and good; and the wedding was furnished with guests. And when the king came in to see the guests, he saw there a man which had not on a wedding-garment. And he saith unto him, Friend, how camest thou in hither, not having a wedding-garment? And he was speechless. Then said the king to the servants, Bind him hand and foot, and take him away, and cast him into outer darkness: there shall be weeping and gnashing of teeth. For many are called, but few are chosen.

The Book of the Gospels.

¶ The Twenty-First Sunday after Trinity.

St. John iv. 46.

THERE was a certain nobleman, whose son was sick at Capernaum. When he heard that Jesus was come out of Judæa into Galilee, he went unto Him, and besought Him that He would come down and heal his son; for he was at the point of death. Then said Jesus unto him, Except ye see signs and wonders, ye will not believe. The nobleman saith unto him, Sir, come down ere my child die. Jesus saith unto him, Go thy way, thy son liveth. And the man believed the word that Jesus had spoken unto him, and he went his way. And, as he was now going down, his servants met him, and told him, saying, Thy son liveth. Then enquired he of them the hour when he began to amend: and they said unto him, Yesterday at the seventh hour the fever left him. So the father knew that it was at the same hour, in the which Jesus said unto him, Thy son liveth; and himself believed, and his whole house. This is again the second miracle that Jesus did, when He was come out of Judæa into Galilee.

The Book of the Gospels.

¶ The Twenty-Second Sunday after Trinity.

St. Matth. xviii. 21.

ETER said unto Jesus, Lord, how oft shall my brother sin against me, and I forgive him? till seven times? Jesus saith unto him, I say not unto thee, until seven times; but until seventy times seven. Therefore is the Kingdom of heaven likened unto a certain king, which would take account of his servants. And when he had begun to reckon, one was brought unto him, which owed him ten thousand talents. But forasmuch as he had not to pay, his lord commanded him to be sold, and his wife and children, and all that he had, and payment to be made. The servant therefore fell down and worshipped him, saying, Lord, have patience with me, and I will pay thee all. Then the lord of that servant was moved with compassion, and loosed him, and forgave him the debt. But the same servant went out, and found one of his fellow-servants, which owed him an hundred pence; and he laid hands on him, and took him by the throat, saying, Pay me that thou owest. And his fellow-servant fell down at his feet, and besought him, saying, Have patience with me, and I will pay thee all. And he would not; but went and cast him into prison, till he should pay the debt. So when his fellow-servants saw what was done, they were very sorry, and came and told unto their lord all that was done. Then his lord, after that he had called him, said unto him, O thou wicked servant, I forgave thee all that debt, because thou desiredst me: shouldest not thou also have had compassion on thy fellow-servant, even as I had pity on thee? And his lord was wroth, and delivered him to the tormentors, till he should pay

The Book of the Gospels.

all that was due unto him. So likewise shall My heavenly Father do also unto you, if ye from your hearts forgive not every one his brother their trespasses.

⁋ The Twenty-Third Sunday after Trinity.

St. Matth. xxii. 15.

THEN went the Pharisees and took counsel how they might entangle Him in His talk. And they sent out unto Him their disciples, with the Herodians, saying, Master, we know that Thou art true, and teachest the way of God in truth, neither carest Thou for any man: for Thou regardest not the person of men. Tell us therefore, What thinkest Thou? Is it lawful to give tribute unto Cæsar, or not? But Jesus perceived their wickedness, and said, Why tempt ye Me, ye hypocrites? shew Me the tribute-money. And they brought unto Him a penny. And He saith unto them, Whose is this image and superscription? They say unto Him, Cæsar's. Then saith He unto them, Render therefore unto Cæsar the things which are Cæsar's; and unto God the things that are God's. When they had heard these words, they marvelled, and left Him, and went their way.

The Book of the Gospels.

❡ The Twenty-Fourth Sunday after Trinity.

St. Matth. ix. 18.

WHILE Jesus spake these things unto John's disciples, behold, there came a certain ruler, and worshipped Him, saying, My daughter is even now dead; but come and lay Thy Hand upon her, and she shall live. And Jesus arose, and followed him, and so did His disciples. (And behold, a woman, which was diseased with an issue of blood twelve years, came behind Him, and touched the hem of His garment; for she said within herself, If I may but touch His garment, I shall be whole. But Jesus turned Him about, and, when He saw her, He said, Daughter, be of good comfort, thy faith hath made thee whole. And the woman was made whole from that hour.) And when Jesus came into the ruler's house, and saw the minstrels and the people making a noise, He said unto them, Give place; for the maid is not dead, but sleepeth. And they laughed Him to scorn. But when the people were put forth, He went in, and took her by the hand, and the maid arose. And the fame hereof went abroad into all that land.

The Book of the Gospels.

¶ The Twenty-Fifth Sunday after Trinity.

St. John vi. 5.

HEN Jesus then lift up His eyes, and saw a great company come unto Him, He saith unto Philip, Whence shall we buy bread that these may eat? (And this He said to prove him; for He Himself knew what He would do.) Philip answered Him, Two hundred pennyworth of bread is not sufficient for them, that every one of them may take a little. One of His disciples, Andrew, Simon Peter's brother, saith unto Him, There is a lad here, which hath five barley-loaves, and two small fishes; but what are they among so many? And Jesus said, Make the men sit down. Now there was much grass in the place. So the men sat down, in number about five thousand. And Jesus took the loaves, and, when He had given thanks, He distributed to the disciples, and the disciples to them that were set down, and likewise of the fishes, as much as they would. When they were filled, He said unto His disciples, Gather up the fragments that remain, that nothing be lost. Therefore they gathered them together, and filled twelve baskets with the fragments of the five barley-loaves, which remained over and above unto them that had eaten. Then those men, when they had seen the miracle that Jesus did, said, This is of a truth that Prophet that should come into the world.

¶ If there be any more Sundays before Advent-Sunday, the Service of some of those Sundays that were omitted after the Epiphany shall be taken in to supply so many as are here wanting. And if there be fewer, the overplus may be omitted: Provided that this last Collect, Epistle, and Gospel shall always be used upon the Sunday next before Advent.

The Book of the Gospels.

¶ Saint Andrew's Day.

St. Matth. iv. 18.

ESUS, walking by the sea of Galilee, saw two brethren, Simon called Peter, and Andrew his brother, casting a net into the sea, (for they were fishers;) and He saith unto them, Follow Me; and I will make you fishers of men. And they straightway left their nets, and followed Him. And going on from thence He saw other two brethren, James the son of Zebedee, and John his brother, in a ship with Zebedee their father, mending their nets; and He called them. And they immediately left the ship and their father, and followed Him.

¶ Saint Thomas the Apostle.

St. John xx. 24.

HOMAS, one of the twelve, called Didymus, was not with them when Jesus came. The other disciples therefore said unto him, We have seen the Lord. But he said unto them, Except I shall see in His Hands the print of the nails, and put my finger into the print of the nails, and thrust my hand into His Side, I will not believe. And after eight days again His disciples were within, and Thomas with them: then came Jesus, the doors being shut, and stood in the midst, and said, Peace be unto you. Then saith He to Thomas, Reach hither thy finger, and behold My Hands; and

The Book of the Gospels.

reach hither thy hand, and thrust it into My Side; and be not faithless, but believing. And Thomas answered and said unto Him, My Lord, and my God. Jesus saith unto him, Thomas, because thou hast seen Me, thou hast believed; blessed are they that have not seen, and yet have believed. And many other signs truly did Jesus in the presence of His disciples, which are not written in this book. But these are written, that ye might believe that Jesus is the Christ, the Son of God; and that believing ye might have life through His Name.

¶ The Conversion of Saint Paul.

St. Matth. xix. 27.

ETER answered and said unto Jesus, Behold, we have forsaken all, and followed Thee; what shall we have therefore? And Jesus said unto them, Verily I say unto you, That ye which have followed Me, in the regeneration when the Son of Man shall sit in the throne of His glory, ye also shall sit upon twelve thrones, judging the twelve tribes of Israel. And every one that hath forsaken houses, or brethren, or sisters, or father, or mother, or wife, or children, or lands, for My Name's sake, shall receive an hundred-fold, and shall inherit everlasting life. But many that are first shall be last, and the last shall be first.

The Book of the Gospels.

THE PRESENTATION OF CHRIST IN THE TEMPLE,

COMMONLY CALLED

¶ The Purification of Saint Mary the Virgin.

[OR CANDLEMASS DAY.]

St. Luke ii. 22.

ND when the days of her Purification, according to the Law of Moses, were accomplished, they brought Him to Jerusalem, to present Him to the Lord; (as it is written in the Law of the Lord, Every male that openeth the womb shall be called holy to the Lord;) and to offer a sacrifice, according to that which is said in the Law of the Lord, A pair of turtle-doves, or two young pigeons. And behold, there was a man in Jerusalem, whose name was Simeon; and the same man was just and devout, waiting for the consolation of Israel: and the Holy Ghost was upon him. And it was revealed unto him by the Holy Ghost, that he should not see death, before he had seen the Lord's Christ. And he came by the Spirit into the temple; and when the parents brought in the Child Jesus, to do for Him after the custom of the Law, then took he Him up in his arms, and blessed God, and said, Lord, now lettest Thou Thy servant depart in peace, according to Thy word: for mine eyes have seen Thy salvation, which Thou hast prepared before the face of all people; a Light to lighten the Gentiles, and the glory of Thy people Israel. And Joseph and His Mother marvelled at those things which were spoken of Him. And Simeon blessed them, and said unto Mary His Mother, Behold, this Child is

The Book of the Gospels.

set for the fall and rising again of many in Israel; and for a sign which shall be spoken against; (yea, a sword shall pierce through thy own soul also;) that the thoughts of many hearts may be revealed. And there was one Anna a prophetess, the daughter of Phanuel, of the tribe of Aser; she was of a great age, and had lived with an husband seven years from her virginity: and she was a widow of about fourscore and four years; which departed not from the temple, but served God with fastings and prayers night and day. And she coming in that instant gave thanks likewise unto the Lord, and spake of Him to all them that looked for redemption in Jerusalem. And when they had performed all things according to the Law of the Lord, they returned into Galilee to their own city Nazareth. And the Child grew, and waxed strong in spirit, filled with wisdom; and the grace of God was upon Him.

¶ Saint Matthias's Day.

St. Matth. xi. 25.

AT that time Jesus answered and said, I thank Thee, O Father, Lord of heaven and earth, because Thou hast hid these things from the wise and prudent, and hast revealed them unto babes. Even so, Father, for so it seemed good in Thy sight. All things are delivered unto Me of My Father: and no man knoweth the Son, but the Father; neither knoweth any man the Father, save the Son, and he to whomsoever the Son will reveal Him. Come unto Me, all ye that labour and are heavy laden, and I will give you rest. Take My yoke upon you, and learn of Me; for I am meek and lowly in heart: and ye shall find rest unto your souls. For My yoke is easy, and My burden is light.

The Book of the Gospels.

❡ The Annunciation of the Blessed Virgin Mary.

St. Luke i. 26.

ND in the sixth month the Angel Gabriel was sent from God unto a city of Galilee named Nazareth, to a Virgin espoused to a man whose name was Joseph, of the house of David; and the Virgin's name was Mary. And the Angel came in unto her, and said, Hail, thou that art highly favoured, the Lord is with thee; blessed art thou among women. And when she saw him she was troubled at his saying, and cast in her mind what manner of salutation this should be. And the Angel said unto her, Fear not, Mary; for thou hast found favour with God. And behold, thou shalt conceive in thy womb, and bring forth a Son, and shalt call His Name JESUS. He shall be great, and shall be called the Son of the Highest; and the Lord God shall give unto Him the throne of His father David. And He shall reign over the house of Jacob for ever; and of His kingdom there shall be no end. Then said Mary unto the Angel, How shall this be, seeing I know not a man? And the Angel answered and said unto her, The Holy Ghost shall come upon thee, and the power of the Highest shall overshadow thee: therefore also that Holy Thing which shall be born of thee shall be called the Son of God. And behold, thy cousin Elizabeth, she hath also conceived a son in her old age; and this is the sixth month with her who was called barren: for with God nothing shall be impossible. And Mary said, Behold the handmaid of the Lord; be it unto me according to thy word. And the Angel departed from her.

The Book of the Gospels.

❦ Saint Mark's Day.

St. John xv. 1.

I AM the true Vine, and My Father is the Husbandman. Every branch in Me that beareth not fruit He taketh away; and every branch that beareth fruit, He purgeth it, that it may bring forth more fruit. Now ye are clean through the word which I have spoken unto you. Abide in Me, and I in you. As the branch cannot bear fruit of itself, except it abide in the vine; no more can ye, except ye abide in Me. I am the Vine, ye are the branches. He that abideth in Me, and I in him, the same bringeth forth much fruit; for without Me ye can do nothing. If a man abide not in Me, he is cast forth as a branch, and is withered; and men gather them, and cast them into the fire, and they are burned. If ye abide in Me, and My words abide in you, ye shall ask what ye will, and it shall be done unto you. Herein is My Father glorified, that ye bear much fruit; so shall ye be My disciples. As the Father hath loved Me, so have I loved you: continue ye in My love. If ye keep My commandments, ye shall abide in My love; even as I have kept My Father's commandments, and abide in His love. These things have I spoken unto you, that My joy might remain in you, and that your joy might be full.

The Book of the Gospels.

¶ Saint Philip and Saint James's Day.

St. John xiv. 1.

ND Jesus said unto His disciples, Let not your heart be troubled; ye believe in God, believe also in Me. In My Father's house are many mansions; if it were not so, I would have told you. I go to prepare a place for you: and if I go and prepare a place for you, I will come again, and receive you unto Myself, that where I am, there ye may be also. And whither I go ye know, and the way ye know. Thomas saith unto Him, Lord, we know not whither Thou goest, and how can we know the way? Jesus saith unto him, I am the Way, the Truth, and the Life: no man cometh unto the Father but by Me. If ye had known Me, ye should have known My Father also: and from henceforth ye know Him, and have seen Him. Philip saith unto Him, Lord, shew us the Father, and it sufficeth us. Jesus saith unto Him, Have I been so long time with you, and yet hast thou not known Me, Philip? He that hath seen Me hath seen the Father; and how sayest thou then, Shew us the Father? Believest thou not that I am in the Father, and the Father in Me? The words that I speak unto you I speak not of Myself; but the Father that dwelleth in Me, He doeth the works. Believe Me, that I am in the Father, and the Father in Me; or else believe Me for the very works' sake. Verily, verily I say unto you, He that believeth on Me, the works that I do shall he do also; and greater works than these shall he do, because I go unto My Father. And whatsoever ye shall ask in My Name, that will I do, that the Father may be glorified in the Son. If ye shall ask any thing in My Name, I will do it.

The Book of the Gospels.

¶ Saint Barnabas the Apostle.

St. John xv. 12.

THIS is My commandment, That ye love one another, as I have loved you. Greater love hath no man than this, that a man lay down his life for his friends. Ye are My friends, if ye do whatsoever I command you. Henceforth I call you not servants; for the servant knoweth not what his lord doeth: but I have called you friends; for all things that I have heard of My Father I have made known unto you. Ye have not chosen Me, but I have chosen you, and ordained you, that ye should go and bring forth fruit, and that your fruit should remain: that whatsoever ye shall ask of the Father in My Name, He may give it you.

¶ Saint John Baptist's Day.

St. Luke i. 57.

ELIZABETH'S full time came that she should be delivered; and she brought forth a son. And her neighbours and her cousins heard how the Lord had shewed great mercy upon her; and they rejoiced with her. And it came to pass, that on the eighth day they came to circumcise the child; and they called him Zacharias, after the name of his father. And his mother answered and said, Not so; but he shall be called John. And they said unto her, There

The Book of the Gospels.

is none of thy kindred that is called by this name. And they made signs to his father, how he would have him called. And he asked for a writing-table, and wrote, saying, His name is John. And they marvelled all. And his mouth was opened immediately, and his tongue loosed, and he spake, and praised God. And fear came on all that dwelt round about them; and all these sayings were noised abroad throughout all the hill-country of Judæa. And all they that had heard them laid them up in their hearts, saying, What manner of child shall this be? And the hand of the Lord was with him. And his father Zacharias was filled with the Holy Ghost, and prophesied, saying, Blessed be the Lord God of Israel: for He hath visited and redeemed His people, and hath raised up an horn of salvation for us in the house of His servant David; as He spake by the mouth of His holy prophets, which have been since the world began; that we should be saved from our enemies, and from the hand of all that hate us: to perform the mercy promised to our fathers, and to remember His holy covenant; the oath which He sware to our father Abraham, that He would grant unto us, that we, being delivered out of the hands of our enemies, might serve Him without fear, in holiness and righteousness before Him all the days of our life. And thou, Child, shalt be called the Prophet of the Highest: for thou shalt go before the face of the Lord to prepare His ways; to give knowledge of salvation unto His people, by the remission of their sins, through the tender mercy of our God, whereby the Day-spring from on high hath visited us: to give light to them that sit in darkness and in the shadow of death, to guide our feet into the way of peace. And the child grew, and waxed strong in spirit; and was in the deserts till the day of his shewing unto Israel.

The Book of the Gospels.

❡ Saint Peter's Day.

St. Matth. xvi. 13.

WHEN Jesus came into the coasts of Cæsarea Philippi, He asked His disciples, saying, Whom do men say that I, the Son of man, am? And they said, Some say that Thou art John the Baptist, some Elias, and others Jeremias, or one of the prophets. He saith unto them, But whom say ye that I am? And Simon Peter answered and said, Thou art Christ, the Son of the living God. And Jesus answered and said unto him, Blessed art thou, Simon Bar-jona: for flesh and blood hath not revealed it unto thee, but My Father Which is in heaven. And I say also unto thee, That thou art Peter, and upon this rock I will build My Church; and the gates of hell shall not prevail against it. And I will give unto thee the keys of the kingdom of heaven: and whatsoever thou shalt bind on earth shall be bound in heaven; and whatsoever thou shalt loose on earth shall be loosed in heaven.

The Book of the Gospels.

¶ Saint James the Apostle.

St. Matth. xx. 20.

HEN came to Him the mother of Zebedee's children with her sons, worshipping Him, and desiring a certain thing of Him. And He said unto her, What wilt thou? She saith unto Him, Grant that these my two sons may sit, the one on Thy right hand, and the other on the left, in Thy Kingdom. But Jesus answered and said, Ye know not what ye ask. Are ye able to drink of the cup that I shall drink of, and to be baptized with the baptism that I am baptized with? They say unto Him, We are able. And He saith unto them, Ye shall drink indeed of My cup, and be baptized with the baptism that I am baptized with: but to sit on My right hand, and on My left, is not Mine to give; but it shall be given to them for whom it is prepared of My Father. And when the ten heard it, they were moved with indignation against the two brethren. But Jesus called them unto Him, and said, Ye know that the princes of the Gentiles exercise dominion over them, and they that are great exercise authority upon them. But it shall not be so among you: but whosoever will be great among you, let him be your minister; and whosoever will be chief among you, let him be your servant: even as the Son of Man came not to be ministered unto, but to minister, and to give His Life a ransom for many.

The Book of the Gospels.

¶ Saint Bartholomew the Apostle.

St. Luke xxii. 24.

AND there was also a strife among them, which of them should be accounted the greatest. And He said unto them, The kings of the Gentiles exercise lordship over them; and they that exercise authority upon them are called benefactors. But ye shall not be so: but he that is greatest among you, let him be as the younger; and he that is chief, as he that doth serve. For whether is greater, he that sitteth at meat, or he that serveth? is not he that sitteth at meat? but I am among you as he that serveth. Ye are they which have continued with Me in My temptations. And I appoint unto you a kingdom, as My Father hath appointed unto Me; that ye may eat and drink at My table in My Kingdom, and sit on thrones judging the twelve tribes of Israel.

¶ Saint Matthew the Apostle.

St. Matth. ix. 9.

AND as Jesus passed forth from thence, He saw a man named Matthew, sitting at the receipt of custom: and He saith unto him, Follow Me. And he arose, and followed Him. And it came to pass, as Jesus sat at meat in the house, behold, many Publicans and sinners came, and sat down with Him and His disciples. And when the Pharisees saw it, they said unto His

The Book of the Gospels.

disciples, Why eateth your Master with Publicans and sinners? But when Jesus heard that, He said unto them, They that be whole need not a physician, but they that are sick. But go ye and learn what that meaneth, I will have mercy, and not sacrifice; for I am not come to call the righteous, but sinners to repentance.

¶ Saint Michael and all Angels.

St. Matth. xviii. 1.

AT the same time came the disciples unto Jesus, saying, Who is the greatest in the Kingdom of heaven? And Jesus called a little child unto Him, and set him in the midst of them, and said, Verily I say unto you, Except ye be converted, and become as little children, ye shall not enter into the Kingdom of heaven. Whosoever therefore shall humble himself as this little child, the same is greatest in the Kingdom of heaven. And whoso shall receive one such little child in My Name, receiveth Me. But whoso shall offend one of these little ones which believe in Me, it were better for him that a milstone were hanged about his neck, and that he were drowned in the depth of the sea. Woe unto the world because of offences: for it must needs be that offences come: but woe to that man by whom the offence cometh. Wherefore if thy hand or thy foot offend thee, cut them off, and cast them from thee: it is better for thee to enter into life halt or maimed, rather than having two hands or two feet to be cast into everlasting fire. And if thine eye offend thee, pluck it out, and cast it from thee: it is better for thee to enter into life with one eye, rather than having two eyes to

The Book of the Gospels.

be cast into hell-fire. Take heed that ye despise not one of these little ones; for I say unto you, That in heaven their Angels do always behold the face of My Father Which is in heaven.

❡ Saint Luke the Evangelist.

St. Luke x. 1.

THE Lord appointed other seventy also, and sent them two and two before His face into every city and place whither He Himself would come. Therefore said He unto them, The harvest truly is great, but the labourers are few; pray ye therefore the Lord of the harvest, that He would send forth labourers into His harvest. Go your ways; behold, I send you forth as lambs among wolves. Carry neither purse, nor scrip, nor shoes, and salute no man by the way. And into whatsoever house ye enter, first say, Peace be to this house. And if the son of peace be there, your peace shall rest upon it: if not, it shall turn to you again. And in the same house remain, eating and drinking such things as they give: for the labourer is worthy of his hire.

The Book of the Gospels.

⁑ Saint Simon and Saint Jude, Apostles.

St. John xv. 17.

THESE things I command you, that ye love one another. If the world hate you, ye know that it hated Me before it hated you. If ye were of the world, the world would love his own: but because ye are not of the world, but I have chosen you out of the world, therefore the world hateth you. Remember the word that I said unto you, The servant is not greater than the lord; if they have persecuted Me, they will also persecute you: if they have kept My saying, they will keep your's also. But all these things will they do unto you for My Name's sake, because they know not Him that sent Me. If I had not come and spoken unto them, they had not had sin: but now they have no cloke for their sin. He that hateth Me hateth My Father also. If I had not done among them the works which none other man did, they had not had sin; but now have they both seen, and hated both Me and My Father. But this cometh to pass, that the word might be fulfilled that is written in their law, They hated Me without a cause. But when the Comforter is come, Whom I will send unto you from the Father, even the Spirit of truth, Which proceedeth from the Father, He shall testify of Me. And ye also shall bear witness, because ye have been with Me from the beginning.

The Book of the Gospels.

❡ All Saints' Day.

St. Matth. v. 1.

ESUS, seeing the multitudes, went up into a mountain; and when He was set, His disciples came unto Him. And He opened His mouth, and taught them, saying, Blessed are the poor in spirit: for their's is the kingdom of heaven. Blessed are they that mourn: for they shall be comforted. Blessed are the meek: for they shall inherit the earth. Blessed are they which do hunger and thirst after righteousness: for they shall be filled. Blessed are the merciful: for they shall obtain mercy. Blessed are the pure in heart: for they shall see God. Blessed are the peace-makers: for they shall be called the children of God. Blessed are they which are persecuted for righteousness' sake: for their's is the kingdom of heaven. Blessed are ye, when men shall revile you, and persecute you, and shall say all manner of evil against you falsely for My sake. Rejoice, and be exceeding glad; for great is your reward in heaven: for so persecuted they the prophets which were before you.

The Book of the Gospels.

❡ At Funerals.

St. John vi. 37.

ESUS said to His disciples and to the multitude, All that the Father giveth Me shall come to Me; and him that cometh to Me I will in no wise cast out. For I came down from Heaven, not to do Mine own will, but the will of Him that sent Me. And this is the Father's will Which hath sent Me, that of all which He hath given Me I should lose nothing, but should raise it up again at the last day. And this is the will of Him that sent Me, that every one which seeth the Son, and believeth on Him, may have everlasting life: and I will raise him up at the last day.

❡ Or else this.

St. John v. 24.

ESUS said to His disciples and to the multitude, Verily, verily, I say unto you, He that heareth My Word, and believeth on Him that sent Me, hath everlasting life, and shall not come into condemnation; but is passed from death unto life. Verily, verily, I say unto you, The hour is coming, and now is, when the dead shall hear the Voice of the Son of God: and they that hear shall live. For as the Father hath life in Himself; so hath He given to the Son to have life in Himself; and hath given Him authority to execute judgment also, because He is the Son of man. Marvel not at this: for the hour is coming, in the which all that are in the graves shall hear His Voice, and shall come forth; they that have done good, unto the resurrection of life; and they that have done evil, unto the resurrection of damnation.

The Book of the Gospels.

❡ The Ordering of Deacons.

St. Luke xii. 35.

ET your loins be girded about, and your lights burning; and ye yourselves like unto men that wait for their Lord, when he will return from the wedding; that, when he cometh and knocketh, they may open unto him immediately. Blessed are those servants, whom the Lord when He cometh shall find watching. Verily I say unto you, that He shall gird Himself, and make them to sit down to meat, and will come forth and serve them. And if He shall come in the second watch, or come in the third watch, and find them so, blessed are those servants.

❡ The Ordering of Priests.

St. Matth. ix. 36.

HEN Jesus saw the multitudes, He was moved with compassion on them, because they fainted, and were scattered abroad as sheep having no shepherd. Then saith He unto His disciples, The harvest truly is plenteous, but the labourers are few. Pray ye therefore the Lord of the harvest, that He will send forth labourers into His harvest.

The Book of the Gospels.

¶ Or else this that followeth, out of the tenth Chapter of St. John.

St. John x. 1.

ERILY, verily I say unto you, He that entereth not by the door into the sheep-fold, but climbeth up some other way, the same is a thief and a robber. But he that entereth in by the door is the Shepherd of the sheep. To him the porter openeth, and the sheep hear his voice; and he calleth his own sheep by name, and leadeth them out. And when he putteth forth his own sheep he goeth before them, and the sheep follow him; for they know his voice. And a stranger will they not follow, but will flee from him; for they know not the voice of strangers. This parable spake Jesus unto them, but they understood not what things they were which He spake unto them. Then said Jesus unto them again, Verily, verily I say unto you, I am the Door of the sheep. All that ever came before Me are thieves and robbers; but the sheep did not hear them. I am the Door; by Me if any man enter in, he shall be saved, and shall go in and out, and find pasture. The thief cometh not but for to steal, and to kill, and to destroy: I am come that they might have life, and that they might have it more abundantly. I am the good Shepherd: the good Shepherd giveth His life for the sheep. But he that is an hireling, and not the Shepherd, whose own the sheep are not, seeth the wolf coming, and leaveth the sheep, and fleeth; and the wolf catcheth them, and scattereth the sheep. The hireling fleeth, because he is an hireling, and careth not for the sheep. I am the good Shepherd, and know My sheep, and am known of Mine. As the Father knoweth Me, even so know I the Father; and I lay down My life for the sheep. And other sheep I have, which are not of this fold: them also I must bring, and they shall hear My voice; and there shall be One Fold, and One Shepherd.

The Book of the Gospels.

¶ The Consecration of Bishops.

St. John xxi. 15.

ESUS saith to Simon Peter, Simon, son of Jonas, lovest thou Me more than these? He saith unto Him, Yea, Lord, Thou knowest that I love Thee. He saith unto him, Feed My lambs. He saith to him again the second time, Simon, son of Jonas, lovest thou Me? He saith unto Him, Yea, Lord, Thou knowest that I love Thee. He saith unto him, Feed My sheep. He saith unto him the third time, Simon, son of Jonas, lovest thou Me? Peter was grieved because He said unto him the third time, Lovest thou Me? And he said unto Him, Lord, Thou knowest all things; Thou knowest that I love Thee. Jesus saith unto him, Feed My sheep.

¶ Or else this.

St. John xx. 19.

HE same day at evening, being the first day of the week, when the doors were shut where the disciples were assembled for fear of the Jews, came Jesus, and stood in the midst, and saith unto them, Peace be unto you. And when He had so said, He shewed unto them His Hands and His Side. Then were the disciples glad, when they saw the Lord. Then saith Jesus to them again, Peace be unto you: as My Father hath sent Me, even so send I you. And when He had said this, He breathed on them, and saith unto them, Receive ye the Holy Ghost. Whosoever sins ye remit, they are remitted unto them; and whosoever sins ye retain, they are retained.

The Book of the Gospels.

¶ Or this.

St. Matth. xxviii. 18.

ESUS came and spake unto them, saying, All power is given unto Me in heaven and in earth. Go ye, therefore, and teach all nations, baptizing them In the Name of the Father, and of the Son, and of the Holy Ghost; teaching them to observe all things whatsoever I have commanded you : and lo, I am with you alway, even unto the end of the world.

¶ The Queen's Accession.

St. Matth. xxii. 16.

ND they sent out unto Him their disciples, with the Herodians, saying, Master, we know that Thou art true, and teachest the way of God in truth, neither carest Thou for any man : for Thou regardest not the person of men. Tell us therefore, What thinkest Thou? Is it lawful to give tribute unto Cæsar, or not? But Jesus perceived their wickedness, and said, Why tempt ye Me, ye hypocrites? shew Me the tribute-money. And they brought unto Him a peny. And He saith unto them, Whose is this image and superscription? They say unto Him, Cæsar's. Then saith He unto them, Render therefore unto Cæsar the things which are Cæsar's; and unto God the things that are God's. When they had heard these words, they marvelled, and left Him, and went their way.

CHISWICK PRESS:—PRINTED BY WHITTINGHAM AND WILKINS,
TOOKS COURT, CHANCERY LANE.

www.ingramcontent.com/pod-product-compliance
Lightning Source LLC
Chambersburg PA
CBHW030408170426
43202CB00010B/1530